We advance our clients
business interests!

↳ We know & understand
our clients business

we protect
our legal structure and
forward a strong
our clients business
interests

We understand each client
& industry

We get it.

→ Reduce w/ provide a
public compan...

   ↳ assigned financing

   ↳ supply chain

   ↳ customer relationship

   ↳ processable for filing
     correct

   ↳ we learn our data
     handle

   ↳ legal solution that address
     Dedicated business

CREATING COMPETITIVE ADVANTAGE

→ supply

⇒ k / supply chain

exports

→ imports in US

→ world trade

CREATING COMPETITIVE ADVANTAGE

GIVE CUSTOMERS A REASON TO CHOOSE YOU OVER YOUR COMPETITORS

JAYNIE L. SMITH

with WILLIAM G. FLANAGAN

CURRENCY DOUBLEDAY

NEW YORK   LONDON   TORONTO   SYDNEY   AUCKLAND

A CURRENCY BOOK
PUBLISHED BY DOUBLEDAY

Copyright © 2006 by Jaynie L. Smith

Book design by Tina Henderson

Cataloging-in-Publication Data is on file with the Library of Congress

ISBN-13: 978-0-385-51709-6
ISBN-10: 0-385-51709-2

PRINTED IN THE UNITED STATES OF AMERICA

SPECIAL SALES
Currency Books are available at special discounts for bulk purchases for sales
promotions or premiums. Special editions, including personalized covers,
excerpts of existing books, and corporate imprints, can be created in large
quantities for special needs. For more information, write to Special Markets,
Currency Books, specialmarkets@randomhouse.com.

9 10

Contents

Acknowledgments

As with any book based on real-life experiences, the cast of participants is the foundation of the work. After years of working with so many wonderful clients as their consultant, coach, and teacher, I have clearly become the student. I would like to thank every client who has given me permission to use their rich experiences and stories in this book so that readers may learn from their failures and successes.

I am eternally grateful for the opportunity to be part of The Executive Committee (TEC), a worldwide organization for CEOs and Key Executives whose mission it is to "improve the effectiveness and enhance the lives of their members." As a TEC Chair for almost seventeen years, I have had the opportunity to help guide the fate of so many companies, thanks to wonderful CEO roundtables and personalized coaching. The positive feedback I have received from TEC members inspired me to write this book, as did my good friend Jeanette Hobson, who graciously kicked me in the butt and inspired me to create a presentation and workshop based on my work.

Fate reconnected me with my friend Bill Flanagan, who so expertly helped to craft *Creating Competitive Advantage*. Not only did he understand and respect my message, he was able to help distill it into a book that is both fun and interesting to read.

My agent, Barbara Lowenstein, was invaluable at every stage of this book's life, from helping us craft an outline, to leading us to a wonderful publisher, to acting as my advocate throughout the publishing process.

Currency Doubleday editorial director Roger Scholl and editor Sarah Rainone were passionate about this project from Day One, and it was their enthusiasm that kept me motivated throughout the process. I would also like to thank Currency deputy publisher Michael Palgon, director of publicity David Drake, publicist Laura Pillar, and associate marketing director Meredith McGinnis for their guidance and support, as well as Rex Bonomelli for creating the book's striking cover. And without Chris Fortunato of Fortunato Book Packaging, and Rebecca Holland, Kate Duffy, Maureen Pickett, and Talia Krohn at Doubleday, this book never would have made it onto the shelves.

Special thanks to my good friend, coach, mentor, and confidant, Ron Fleisher, who got me through so many trials and tribulations I cannot count them all.

Finally, I thank Craig Mowrey, my partner and best friend, for all his help rereading chapters when I couldn't see the forest for the trees and adding editing touches I completely missed. He knows my work inside-out, and he added perspective when it was most needed.

CREATING COMPETITIVE ADVANTAGE

CHAPTER 1

Competitive Advantage Is the Reason You're in Business

COMPETITIVE ADVANTAGE IS WHAT SEPARATES YOU from the rest of the herd. It's what keeps your business alive and growing. In short, it's the reason you are in business. Yet the biggest marketing flaw in most companies is their failure to fully reap the benefits of their competitive advantages. Either they think they have a competitive advantage but don't. Or they have one and don't even realize it. Or they know they have a strong competitive advantage but fail to promote it adequately to their customers and prospects.

In my research with middle-market companies, I found only two CEOs out of 1,000 who could clearly name their companies' competitive advantages. The other

99.8 percent could offer only vague, imprecise generalities. These same CEOs often rely on outside consultants to guide strategic planning sessions. Yet, in my experience, very few consultants—even seasoned ones—give competitive advantage evaluation more than a superficial glance. Why? I wonder. And no matter the size of your company or the kind of business you are in, your competitive advantages should be the foundation of *all* your strategic and operational decisions. Ignoring them can be an expensive and even fatal mistake. After all, they're the reason customers choose to buy from you instead of the other guy. Without this edge, you will lose customers. Eventually, you will go out of business.

On the other hand, if you properly identify and exploit your competitive advantage, it will impact your bottom line early and often. Because your competitive advantage can be your *deal closer*. It answers the customer's key question: Why should I do business with you? What are you offering that the other guy doesn't?

If you can articulate a clear, specific reply to that question, you have your competitive advantage. If you can't, this book will show you how.

THE BIGGEST THREAT IS THE ONE YOU DON'T SEE

It's easy for today's business managers to lose sight of the basics as they focus their attention on a host of other reasons why their margins may be shrinking. You read and hear a lot about the threats of offshore outsourcing. You worry about falling behind in your use of new communications tools and in making the most of the Internet. These threats are certainly real, but you'll never have to deal with them if a more basic problem undermines your company.

In the U.S. Army, young recruits are taught this life-or-death lesson during combat field training. The recruits are alerted that three snipers (played by other soldiers) are crawling through the grass toward them.

As they wait for the aggressors to advance, suddenly, across the field, a figure pops up, and the recruits begin firing (using blanks). A little closer in, another figure pops up, and again the recruits direct their fire to that target. Two seconds later, the platoon is "annihilated" by hand grenades tossed by the third aggressor, who has managed to sneak up right next to the platoon while they fired at distant targets. The platoon was "wiped out" because it failed to act against the closest, and therefore the most serious, threat.

As a business manager or owner, the biggest threat you face is losing sight of your most important target—your customer. He is the one who can blow up your business simply by going elsewhere. You may play golf with him, bend over backward to rush a delivery to him, and even consider him a friend. But you can lose him to a competitor if you lose sight of your competitive advantage.

Too often, managers who see their businesses drifting and their margins shrinking will try to compete based on price. But the manager who drops his prices while his market share is shrinking is courting tragedy. It's like that old joke: "He's losing $3 on every shirt he sells, but he hopes to make it up on volume."

YOU'RE NOT WAL-MART

Most businesses cannot exist by being the lowest-cost providers. Wal-Mart can, but you probably can't. Still, too many companies allow price to be their only differentiator. They tout their prices even in the era of the Internet, where the click of a mouse almost always leads to a lower price. All those companies racing to the bottom are ignoring this vital fact: Price isn't everything. When you compete on price, you're accepting commodity status.

In my work with clients, we do not even discuss price. Play the price game and you are tossing margins to the wind. You become a commodity supplier rather than a marketer, and unless you enjoy vast economies of scale like Wal-Mart, you'll eventually find yourself whistling through the graveyard.

There are other ways to help your customers cut costs that have nothing to do with lowering your prices. If your products and services are more reliable, you can save customers costly downtime. Your service might be worth more because you provide it 24/7. Your products might be worth more because they are demonstrably better than the other guy's—or because you are the only company in the business that offers guarantees, free installation, free replacement, or employee training. Packaging, too, can make a critical difference.

To remain competitive, you have to become more conscious about why you are in business in the first place and what you are delivering that makes you unique. In the following pages, I will show you how you can continually increase your sales and profits by identifying and maximizing your competitive advantages. It's a basic, proven concept that will dramatically increase the number of deals that you close. Warning: It may force you to rethink the way you compete.

My "formula" applies to all companies regardless of product or service, size, or volume. It doesn't matter if you are selling fish sticks, furniture design, or financial services. Customers are customers.

BEEP—YOUR TABLE IS READY

One of my favorite small-company success stories is JTECH, a company that created a paging system for restaurants. If you have ever walked into an Outback Steakhouse, you are familiar with JTECH's product. It's a nifty, coaster-size pager that alerts you when your table is ready. Developed back in the 1980s, the paging system was the brainchild of Dave Miller and Jeff Graham. Graham was an investor and Miller a partner and operating manager of a barn-size restaurant named Mr. Laffs, located on the Intracoastal Waterway in Jensen Beach, Florida. The place was doing very well and one busy Sunday seated a record 1,100 people, who spent a combined $40,000 that day.

A few days later, Miller was out on the golf course with some friends, feeling pretty good about himself and his business, until his pals darkened his mood. They all frequented Mr. Laffs, and they were not happy.

"It's too long a wait for a table," one friend told him. "I had to walk out."

Miller felt as if his wallet had been stolen. Walkaways are to a restaurant manager what casualties are to a general in combat. You lose enough of them, and your fighting days are over. Walkaways not only represent immediate loss of business; they spread the bad word that you can't get a table, so don't bother trying. In the immortal words of Yogi Berra, when describing the original Mr. Laffs in New York City, "Nobody goes there anymore, it's too crowded."

Miller and his partners had a serious problem. Diners often had to wait too long to be seated, so some customers walked. Yet even as some folks were strolling out of the place, tables were becoming free all over the sprawling restaurant. There had to be a better way of getting fannies to the tables, and keeping customers happy enough to wait when necessary.

Graham, a former executive with Pratt & Whitney, along with Miller and their team, proposed using a basic paging system so the staff could communicate better.

Using an old Atari game cartridge, a pager housing a computer, and radio frequency technology they had developed in a prior venture, the team cobbled together a simple on-site paging system. Waiters and managers carried the pagers and devised codes for different messages. One beep might mean a table was ready for seating, for example. Two beeps meant food was ready for pickup. Three beeps indicated a dirty table, four beeps that there was an upset customer.

"It was primitive, but it worked," Miller recalls. "We had fewer walkaways. It made a difference."

It made an even bigger difference when Mr. Laffs began handing out its pagers to the customers themselves. Instead of nervously hanging around the hostess desk, listening for their names to be called or flashed on an unsightly screen, diners could relax at the bar and wait for their beepers to flash or vibrate to announce that their tables were ready. "Customers knew we weren't about to ignore them, since they had our beepers," Miller said.

The paging system soon paid for itself many times over. Within months, other restaurant owners in the area were asking about the system and how they could acquire one. Meantime, Miller and Graham kept tinkering with improvements and refinements. It didn't take long for them to realize that they had a potentially dynamite business on their hands. They took off their aprons and started JTECH Wireless Solutions, supplying paging systems to restaurants and other businesses.

Despite some early successes, JTECH had trouble

convincing major restaurant chains to invest in the new system. So Miller and his sales team did cost analyses to show how the new system slashed the number of walkaways and otherwise increased efficiency. The chains listened harder. They tested the new system. And eventually, they bought it.

Houston's, which then had some thirty-five outlets, signed on. Outback Steakhouses, then with sixty-five stores, soon followed suit. Other chains and major independent restaurants followed: Darden Restaurants, Brinker International, Longhorn Steakhouse, TGI Friday's, Legal Seafood, PF Chang's China Bistro, Champps Americana, Panera Bread, Schlotzkey's Deli, Atlanta Bread Company, Angus Barn, Tavern on the Green, and Scoma's.

JTECH was on a roll. By this time, Miller and his partners had leased their restaurant and were involved full-time with their increasingly sophisticated paging systems, looking for new markets beyond the restaurant trade. Soon the business expanded to the entire hospitality industry, from restaurants and hotels to bars, nightclubs, casinos, country clubs, and cruise ships. New markets popped up like mushrooms after a hard rain, not always where expected.

Automobile dealers and auto service centers began signing up, as well. They used the system to locate sales staff faster, to improve communications among staff, and to alert customers when their cars were finished with servicing.

Best Buy, the giant electronics chain with close to 700 outlets, now hands out JTECH beepers to customers while they wait for their computer systems to be configured, upgraded, or repaired. Target stores, with more than 1,100 stores in forty-seven states, has been supplying JTECH pagers to customers waiting for drug prescriptions to be filled at their in-store pharmacies. While they wait, they shop.

"We started getting calls every Monday from Baptist churches," Miller says. "They wanted to use paging systems in their nurseries to signal parents. We could never figure out why we got so many of those calls on Mondays, until we realized that churchgoers were seeing the system at work in restaurant chains over the weekend. They saw its potential for their own churches and promptly called us on Monday mornings."

Hospitals and health care providers began calling. Dozens of shopping malls became customers—especially at Christmas, when kids come to see Santa. When the elves are nearly ready to bring the kids to the big guy, parents get paged. Miller even had a request to develop a system to help train Dalmatians. Many of the breed are deaf, making then hard to train. But JTECH developed a small handheld transmitter that gives off a gentle vibration to prompt the dog to look at its trainer to heed hand signals.

JTECH was doing fine, but soon it had competition. A few other companies popped up around the country offering the same kind of device. Eventually, Motorola waded in. "Motorola made a serious run at this business in 1995 and 1996," Miller recalls. After all, the name Motorola was practically synonymous with pagers.

"We had been in business for years, and we felt we knew the needs of our customers better than Motorola or anyone else. But how could we prove it on the spot to a new customer?"

It was a nagging question, as Motorola wasn't the only company jealously eyeing JTECH's growth. What could JTECH say that made it better than the competition? Unsure of the answer, in 1999, Jeff Graham, then president of the company, called me and scheduled one of my workshops on competitive advantage.

At the workshop, JTECH executives set about determining exactly what the company's strongest competitive advantage was. Its service was great, its equipment top of the line, its costs competitive. But that's what the competition said, too. JTECH needed a simple, strong, accurate, and convincing statement to differentiate itself from its competitors.

The JTECH team brainstormed at the workshop and afterward to determine and articulate JTECH's best competitive advantage—in straightforward, quantifiable terms. They kicked it around among themselves, asked their customers, and finally nailed it down:

 Of the fifty largest chains who use paging, 100 percent use JTECH.

That one statement was better than a royal warrant—it put the competition on the ropes. Restaurant chains are notoriously tough sells, but JTECH had won them over and kept them on. JTECH quickly adopted the slogan and made it a mantra. Customers responded. Sales closed faster. Competitors couldn't counter that message.

"People who make the decisions to invest in things like the paging system cannot afford to make mistakes," Graham says. "The statement that the top fifty major chains used JTECH absolutely removed the risk from the buying decisions for new store owners, and price became much less of an issue."

In 2004, JTECH had its best year, with sales topping $20 million. In 2005, the owners sold out to MICROS Systems, a supplier of information technology to the hospitality industry, but continue to operate as a wholly owned subsidiary. So the founders have cashed in and still continue to operate the business.

WINNING BIG WITH BIG BERTHA

Is there a Big Bertha in your golf bag? Chances are there is, if you play a lot of golf and are willing to spend a few hundred dollars on a single club that might improve your game.

When Ely Callaway, the founder of Callaway Golf, decided to get into the golf equipment business, he knew he needed to offer something special to the legions of hapless duffers, like me, who were desperate to lower their scores. He knew that golf truly is a triumph of hope over experience.

Callaway knew that most golfers rarely break 100. He also knew that nothing makes a duffer feel better than smashing a long, straight drive off the tee, even if the rest of his or her game is lousy.

The year was 1982, and Callaway had already succeeded in two very different careers. He was sixty-three years old, an age when most men play golf rather than make it a business. He'd been CEO of the textile giant Burlington Industries and then started his own winery in Southern California, Callaway Wines, which he sold in order to buy an obscure maker of golf equipment. By 1997, Callaway was the largest manufacturer of golf clubs in America, with sales of $843 million, largely thanks to his Big Bertha drivers.

Callaway Golf has been such an enormous success because its founder aimed right from the outset to give his company a leg up on the competition that couldn't quickly be matched. Innovation was part of the company's business plan right from the beginning. The Big Bertha used new technology, materials, and design and was vigorously promoted. Did Big Bertha drivers actually allow duffers to play better golf? Ely Callaway always danced around that question, posed by a *BusinessWeek* reporter. "If our golf clubs didn't assist the average golfer in hitting more pleasing shots, then why do we sell as many as we do?" Callaway coyly responded.

By the time competitors began manufacturing their own oversize, high-tech metal drivers to compete with the Big Bertha, Callaway was already on the green. To keep his competitive advantage, Callaway kept on improving his Big Bertha (named after the huge cannon employed by the Germans during World War 1 to bombard Paris). On the heels of the success of Big Bertha, Callaway came up with a Great Big Bertha, and finally Biggest Big Bertha, the head of which looks like a curling stone. Callaway introduced full sets of pricey, high-tech irons, sumptuous leather bags and accessories, and even began making Callaway golf balls. He and his designers kept the USGA, the sanctioning body for golf equipment, very busy evaluating the legality of his high-tech gear.

At the time of his death in July 2001, Callaway was still busy forging innovations in equipment, making acquisitions, and promoting the Callaway name. He fed the perception that Callaways will improve your game.

But the company hardly died with him. Ely Callaway had built a strong management team and a corporate culture that have continued to keep the Callaway ball rolling. His innovative equipment was the company's biggest external competitive advantage, but it didn't stop there. Callaway had also instilled a culture of innovation in his company. This is why the company is still a leader in the industry.

Here is how the company describes itself: "Callaway Golf Company designs, creates, builds, and sells Demonstrably Superior and Pleasingly Different golf products. That means that any club, ball, or putter in the Callaway Golf family must be a significant improvement not only upon the products of our competitors, but also our own."

EXXONMOBIL: A SEISMIC ADVANTAGE

There are two kinds of competitive advantage, in my view—external and internal. External competitive advantages include patented products or outstanding service that competitors cannot match. External competitive advantages are highly visible to the buyer—or should be. But companies also have internal competitive advantages. They are not visible to the customer but can give a company a big edge on the competition. Examples of internal competitive advantages include Wal-Mart's buying power and Coca-Cola's distribution. (Later in this book, I will also discuss something I call competitive positioning. This involves making a substantial statement that may not be an actual competitive advantage, but might still give you an edge because you make the claim before—or more effectively than—anyone else.)

The oil industry is not an arena where external competitive advantages would seem to be important. Oil and gas are commodities, after all, and the OPEC cartel largely succeeds in controlling supply. As a result, the giants ExxonMobil, Chevron Texaco, British Petroleum, and Royal Dutch Petroleum don't really have to compete, it would seem, so much as quietly divvy up the world's markets. Oil is oil, gas is gas, and one brand is the same as another.

But despite the coziness of the suppliers and the OPEC cartel, oil companies do indeed compete. One of the most critical areas in which they compete is oil and gas exploration. New finds mean fatter profits. But it has become increasingly difficult to find fields that can be easily tapped. Ironically, most oil companies spent less money on research and development in 2004 than they did a decade earlier—even with oil prices at record levels. They focused on near-term profits and left the costly and risky business of developing new search technologies to oil drilling and service companies. Deep-water wells— where many of the most promising new fields are located—can cost upward of $70 million each, and still come up empty. Hit a few dry wells at those prices and profits can evaporate faster than gasoline.

ExxonMobil was worried about the lack of technological advancement in the field of oil discovery. Seismic surveying had been widely used to find new fields, but that technology—which uses sound waves to find likely oil spots—doesn't work well in deep water. And it is in deep water—3,000 feet and more—where the most promising locations are found: off the coasts of Russia and Africa, and in the Gulf of Mexico.

But ExxonMobil didn't have its head in the sand. For years, the company had a geophysicist on its payroll who had quietly been working on a new way to probe for deposits in very deep water, Dr. Len Srnka. Srnka, who once worked for NASA, was studying the electromagnetic properties of earth, water, and rock in order to find oil. Srnka even patented his system, called R3M (remote reservoir resistivity) in the late 1980s, but it was shelved in favor of the proven seismic methods, which were constantly being improved.

When the oil giant got wind that a small oil company, Norway's Statoil, was also experimenting with electromagnetic technology, it gave the green light to Dr. Srnka to conduct field trials using R3M. A few years, lots of trials, and many millions of dollars later, ExxonMobil is now using Srnka's R3M technology to help unlock hidden oil deposits in the deep sea, giving it an enormous potential advantage in discovering more deposits.

"If Exxon is right," said the *Wall Street Journal* in reporting the story, "it could give the world's largest publicly traded oil company a competitive advantage over its rivals."

LOOKING FOR YOUR
COMPETITIVE ADVANTAGE EDGE

It doesn't take the savvy of the founders of JTECH, or the genius of Ely Callaway, or the deep pockets of an ExxonMobil to grasp the importance of competitive advantage. Every company in the world wants an edge on the competition; ironically, few are willing to do what it takes to get that edge.

Competitive advantage goes by other names, as well: Unique selling position. Distinguishing features. Competitive edge. Discriminators. Differentiators. In 1985, Michael E. Porter wrote a groundbreaking textbook on the subject, *Competitive Advantage: Creating and Sustaining Superior Performance*. Then a young teacher at the Harvard Business School, Porter articulated many ways in which companies could devise, identify, and maximize their competitive advantages.

Basically, Porter stated that a competitive advantage can come about in two ways—cost advantage and differentiation advantage. The first is obvious, and hardly revolutionary. If you charge less than the other guy for the same goods and services, you have a decided advantage. That's why America shops at Wal-Mart. But, as we have seen, being the lowest-cost producer isn't often possible or desirable for most businesses. Just ask the executives at Kmart about its disastrous "Blue-Light Specials." The company tried to undersell Wal-Mart and lost so much money it went into bankruptcy. Now, as part of Sears Holdings Corporation, it continues to close stores and slash personnel. It isn't enough to stay alive—you have to make a profit.

It is in differentiation, however, that the vast majority of successful businesses find their competitive advantages. Target stores thrive in the shadow of Wal-Mart by offering higher-quality goods (at higher prices). Designer boutiques thrive by selling designer merchandise (at even higher prices).

Technology is often the source of differentiation advantages—but only for a time. Ely Callaway made a bigger and better golf club using space-age materials and innovative design. Exxon sank a fortune into electromagnetic search technology while most of its rivals yawned.

But, remember, technology now moves at the speed of summer lightning. The days when a Xerox Corp. or an IBM could enjoy decades of superiority because of its patented technology are over. Patents can offer some protection to truly innovative companies, but not nearly as much as in the heyday of Xerox and IBM.

DON'T TRUST THE PATENT OFFICE

Witness Microsoft, which has pioneered precious few products for a corporation of its enormous size. Windows, its most celebrated product, features technology first developed by Xerox Corp., something called a "graphic-user interface." The company proudly showed it off to young entrepreneur Steve Jobs, and shortly thereafter his Apple computers featured GUI in a form now familiar to computer users worldwide. Jobs borrowed from Xerox, and Microsoft borrowed from Apple.

Who really owns the process? That's for patent attorneys to fight over. "Patent infringement" is not something that seems to bother many of today's high-tech firms. So differentiating your company by using a new technology is only likely to give you a temporary edge in today's marketplace.

The best competitive advantage is a sustainable one. Callaway Golf would likely have faded faster than one of my errant tee shots if its only competitive advantage was Big Bertha. Coca-Cola would not be the successful giant it is today if it relied on its secret formula. (Most people still can't tell the difference between Coke and Pepsi in one-on-one taste tests; in fact, they usually pick Pepsi, probably because it is 4 percent sweeter.)

Callaway's competitors eventually introduced their own oversize metal drivers, which meant Big Bertha alone was not a sustainable competitive advantage. Nor were Bigger Bertha and Great Big Bertha. But what Callaway had developed was a reputation for being cutting edge, for developing products that improve your game—or at least make it more enjoyable.

Similarly, Coca-Cola's secret formula isn't what makes the company great today. It is its ability to supply the thirsty consumer with any kind of non-alcoholic beverage he or she wants, from orange juice to bottled water, anywhere from Times Square to Rangoon. Its sales, marketing, bottling, and distribution—internal competitive advantages— are what really differentiate the company. (Small wonder that Warren Buffett, a vocal proponent of competitive advantage, is a board member and major stockholder.)

Competitive advantage is more than just manufacturing a better mousetrap, golf club, or carbonated beverage. In his book *Gaining & Sustaining Competitive Advantage,* Jay B. Barney came up with this textbook definition:

> A firm is said to have a sustained competitive advantage when it is implementing a value-creating strategy not simultaneously being implemented by any current or potential competitors and when these firms are unable to duplicate the benefits of this strategy.

That's quite a mouthful, but you get the idea. If you are the owner or manager of a business, your mind is now probably racing trying to pin down your own company's competitive advantages. But remember this: Most companies do indeed have them (or had them) or they wouldn't be in business in the first place. But even if you don't, you can invent them. I will show you how in Chapter 9.

I have done workshops on competitive advantage for thousands of executives. Once we have discussed the basics and gone over some examples, I ask my audience, "Did anyone come up with something you have not used before in your marketing and sales efforts?" Nearly everyone shoots up a hand. They can hardly wait to run out of the room to start using their newly discovered competitive advantages. I can count on one hand the number of companies among the hundreds I've worked with who did not walk away with "newly discovered" competitive advantages after the workshop sessions. But this is when I caution them to slow down. Before touting your competitive advantages all over town, you have to *run them by your customers first*. After all, you could be wrong in your assumptions about what they value as important. In fact, my experience has taught me that there's a good chance that you are off the mark. Your customers may not share your opinion of what is so special about your company. Or worse, the so-called advantages that you tout may even turn them away. I call this disconnect "dangerous disparity," and I will discuss it further in Chapter 7.

IDENTIFYING YOUR
COMPETITIVE ADVANTAGES

Your eventual goal should be to come up with a hard list of competitive advantages that you can use to increase profits at your company. So get out pen and paper, or spark up your laptop, and write down the answers to the questions below. Let your imagination go. Bounce your answers off colleagues, if you like, just as I ask people to do in my workshops. In fact, it is better if you involve your top staff as well as others from different departments. The more ideas, the better. At this point, you want a long laundry list of possible competitive advantages, which you will refine, winnow, reject, and rethink as you progress through the book.

Note: You might settle on a single, clear competitive advantage with which to go to war. Or you might have five to ten or more competitive advantages with which to arm your sales staff. Sometimes a single shot will level your enemy; sometimes it takes a machine gun.

But before you begin, some words of caution. As you make up your list, bear in mind the following:

Competitive advantage is objective, not subjective. How many times do we hear a company say, "You should do business with us because we deliver good quality and great customer service"? Well, your idea of quality and my idea of quality may be galaxies apart. This kind of boast is subjective and tells us nothing. In fact, words like quality, reputation, and trust, when used to describe competitive advantage, are so hackneyed we tune them out.

It is quantifiable, not arbitrary. Which statement is more compelling: "We have great customer service" or "Ninety-five percent of our business comes from referrals"? When you make objective, quantifiable statements such as these, the customer is more likely to believe your claims. Your company may be trustworthy, loyal, helpful, friendly, courteous, kind, obedient, cheerful, thrifty, brave, clean, and reverent. And your customers may appreciate those traits. But they don't buy from you for your Boy Scout traits. In fact, in today's marketplace, they have come to expect them as givens.

It isn't claimed by the competition. If your sales force goes out with a list of attributes that your competitors can match or exceed, you are courting disaster. (In fact, that is the principal reason so many sales calls don't result in closings or why salespeople resort to price as a tiebreaker.) Find out exactly what you provide that the other guy doesn't and harp on it. Explore what that advantage means to the customer. If it can save him money—and it often can—make sure you stress that. Better yet, tell the customer how much he saves by using you. Even if your goods or services are more expensive than those of the competition, you can still save your customers money because of fewer breakdowns, guaranteed on-time delivery, training assistance, better payment terms, and so on.

It is not a cliché. Don't tell me that you "exceed your customer's expectations." How do you know what their expectations are? Your customers expect good service. How do they define good service, and how do you? I bet those definitions are not the same. After all, who would admit to providing bad service? Again, be specific. If you provide service twenty-four hours a day, seven days a week—and the others guys don't—say so.

Now you're ready to start writing:

- What are your company's most critical competitive advantages?
- What do your employees think are your company's competitive advantages?
- What are your competitors' competitive advantages?
- How do you respond to customers when they ask, "Why should I buy from you?"

CHAPTER 2

How Competitive Advantage Closes Deals

D<small>AVID</small> M<small>AMET</small>'<small>S</small> <small>BRILLIANT PLAY</small> *G<small>LENGARRY</small> G<small>LEN</small> Ross* is all about salesmen closing deals. If you've seen the film version, you'll recall that Alec Baldwin plays a ruthless, foulmouthed sales manager who berates, mocks, and threatens to fire his sales staff for failing to close on land deals in Arizona and Florida. He stages a contest that awards a brand-new Cadillac to the salesman who closes the most deals in the next few days. Second place is a set of steak knives. The other salesmen face getting pink slips.

The salesmen are good—very good. Jack Lemmon's character in the film could charm the devil himself. But after all the schmooze, hype, sizzle, and pressure, the veteran salesmen are still unable to close deals. Why? Because they say very little about the land they are selling, only that the customer has to act right now to take advantage of a once-in-a-lifetime opportunity.

Instead, they scheme to get their hands on a fresh list of sales leads. They are going for what I call the shotgun approach—shoot enough bullets and you're bound to hit something. The more leads, the better the odds.

EVEN THE BEST SALESPEOPLE CAN'T CLOSE ROTTEN DEALS

There are only so many suckers out there. It takes a truly gifted salesperson to sell unseen swampland in Florida. On the other hand, it doesn't take a superstar to close a deal that the customer wants. All it takes is a script of your competitive advantages. After all, remember, your competitive advantages answer the customer's most crucial question: Why should I buy from you? If you can persuasively answer that question, your deal is closed.

And who is asked that question most often? Your sales force. As your front line, they should be able to answer that question in spades. But too often they don't know, haven't been told, or don't pay enough attention to your competitive advantages. My work with companies has confirmed that most salespeople are using the old clichés to tout their companies' advantages. When I ask ten sales-people in one company, "Why us?" I often get ten different answers. To top that off, the CEO often has his or her own version, different from that of the sales force. And none of the responses answers the question "Why us?"

When I was in the market for a new car recently, I thought I would have an easy time of it, because I knew exactly what I wanted—a full-size car (not an SUV) that has a top safety rating. To me, safety comes first. After that, I consider styling, mileage, resale value, and so on. That's why I had been driving Volvos for years. Volvos consistently score high in safety with the National Highway Traffic Safety Administration, which does crash tests and other safety evaluations. But surely, I thought as I was shopping for a new car, other automakers would have made their cars safer in recent years, too. Federal regulations have gotten tougher, and smart consumers know that cars with high safety ratings can give you better protection in an accident, and have lower insurance costs and higher resale values.

So I visited four dealerships that offered models I was interested in—pending their safety ratings. I spoke to salespeople at Lexus, Infiniti, Honda, and Acura dealerships. They were all very attentive, but surprisingly ignorant about the cars they were selling. I asked each of them, "What does this car have that others don't?" In other words, what were its competitive advantages? I got blank stares in response.

"Take it for a drive—you'll love the way it drives," said

one salesperson. As a former New Yorker whose idea of a good ride was a yellow cab, I had no doubt that the car would be a pleasure to drive, but that is hardly a unique selling proposition. He might as well have told me that it smelled nice.

My money question followed: "What about safety ratings?" Not a single salesperson could answer me. One even muttered, "If you drive a Volvo, we can't compete."

All of the salespeople I spoke to blew it. None of them could close a deal, because none of them knew enough about the cars they were selling. I am still driving a Volvo, because I haven't found anyone to give me a compelling reason to drive anything else. Moral: It doesn't matter how attentive or charming your salespeople are if they can't close deals. Closing deals involves much more than the power of persuasion, or last-minute sales gimmickry. To get a signature on a contract, your sales force has to be able to answer the question: What's so special about your product or service?

Note: When I made my most recent purchase, not even the Volvo salesman was totally up to speed on the car's latest safety features. I had to read the owner's manual to discover features the salesman never mentioned, including a whiplash protection system, brake circuit redundancy, traction and spin control, and so on. Luckily for him, I had done my homework. But think how many potential customers he might have lost by failing to mention those features.

IT TAKES THE GOODS
TO BE A GOOD CLOSER

One client of mine, the CEO of an interior design firm, was troubled by his staff's inability to close deals. His twenty-two interior designers were delivering prospects, but the CEO had to close every deal himself. He had to spend so much time on closings that he was almost burned out. So he asked me to help convert his designers into salespeople who could close their own deals.

I give a lot of credit to the CEO/owner for recognizing that he needed to spend less time on matters that his staff could handle. Too many CEOs spend too much time *in* their businesses instead of *on* their businesses. The CEO should act as captain up on the bridge, directing the ship, keeping an eye on the horizon for new targets, and steering clear of the icebergs. He shouldn't be stoking coal in the boiler room, or tending lines.

Jim Collins drives this point home in his bestseller *Good to Great*. He calls the best top executives "Level 5 leaders." "Level 5 leaders channel their ego needs away from themselves and into the larger goal of building a great company," he writes. "It's not that Level 5 leaders have no ego or self-interest. Indeed, they are incredibly ambitious—*but their ambition is first and foremost for the institution, not themselves.*"

It shouldn't be surprising that Bill Gates insists upon taking a week off each year to sit in a lakeside cabin, think about his company's future, and read and evaluate employee ideas and proposals. His annual retreat stirs his imagination and gives him a chance to look at the bigger picture. After all, if he doesn't do it, who will?

For my client to be able to spend more time on his business, he had to turn his designers into closers. But we knew they were not professional salespeople and would require a lot of sales training. There are plenty of sales schools that the CEO could have turned to, but they can be expensive and time-consuming and would keep his designers away from customers for too long.

We decided that the best solution was to arm the designers with one sales tool they'd be sure to use—the company's competitive advantages. When it came time to close, the designers would point out those advantages to their clients and seal the deals without having to call on the CEO.

My client and I scheduled a Saturday workshop session at a conference center near his company's offices and alerted his staff to set the date aside for the all-day encounter. At the workshop session, the CEO and his design team spouted lots of reasons why customers should use his company. The principal reasons they cited were that the company employed talented designers and teams, offered one-stop shopping, guaranteed its work, had a strong infrastructure, and provided good service.

Yes, but what did all those qualities really mean to customers? Every design firm in town was promising the same things. What was so special about this one?

The firm certainly had a lot to brag about—from industry awards to high-profile, repeat commercial clients. It also boasted an impressive list of individual homeowners who were so satisfied with the quality of the work that they became repeat customers. They trusted the firm to meet deadlines, and they were not disappointed.

Our task was to quantify these special qualities so they wouldn't sound like empty generalities to potential customers. After drilling down a lot deeper into their accomplishments during the workshop session, the designers came up with competitive advantages and competitive positioning statements that were a lot more specific, meaningful, and persuasive to customers.

Key among them was the fact that the company stays on budget 95 percent of the time. This is critical to clients, especially commercial clients. For developers, the firm also offered these competitive advantages:

- It employed the only design team chosen by the top ten luxury developers in the state.
- Real-estate developers' sales ratios rose by 35 percent after using the firm.
- A computer-assisted design saves up to ten days in project scheduling and allows for same-day changes.
- It was the only firm providing daily job supervision with on-site project managers.

For homeowners, the firm offered these competitive advantages to consider:

- Ninety-eight percent of our designs entered in design competitions won awards—a total of fifty-nine in the past ten years.
- The firm's debt-free stability assures that vendors and contractors show up on time. (They know they will be paid on time, so they show up on time.)
- The firm's designers have an average of twenty-three years' design experience and are available twenty-four hours a day, six days a week.
- Ninety percent of residential clients come from referrals or are repeat customers.

The CEO reports that since the firm identified and began touting these competitive advantages to clients, the firm's closing rate has climbed 30 percent. Not only are the designers able to close deals, they are closing more of them than the CEO could manage himself. And they didn't need any expensive sales training to learn how.

A REAL ESTATE BROKER
WITH A DIFFERENCE

The more your customers know about your competitive advantages, the more deals you'll close. So make sure they find out.

After several decades in commercial real estate, Paul Lehrer grew tired of running his business, which included supervising a full-service staff of fifty. So he sold the business and retired. His retirement lasted for less than three months. "Marge, my wife, kicked me out of the house," he jokes. "She wanted her eight-to-six time back. So I repackaged myself as a corporate real estate advisor."

From all his years in the business, Lehrer knew that the playing field was full of brokers anxious to represent landlords and sellers, but that corporations were usually left on their own, or were represented by a broker who was working for the adversary. The brokers who showed them properties were much more interested in the commissions than in satisfying the needs of the corporate user, the buyer, or the tenant.

So Lehrer and his partner, Michael Feuerman, began a firm, Lehrer & Feuerman, that would represent corporate users in their real estate transactions and charge hourly or per-task fees, in most cases, instead of commissions.

"Our mission was to only take on that portion of commercial real estate which I found to be the most challenging, creative, exciting, and fun. We only wanted twenty-five clients each," Lehrer says. "Our target prospect was the small to midcap employer, where decisions were made within the C suite, not in a real estate department. C suite executives traditionally aren't caught up in 'safe choices.'"

Lehrer knew that he would have to do a lot more than hang out a shingle, send out an announcement, and call some of his contacts. He had to reposition himself as a corporate real estate advisor and convince clients that he could save them a lot more than the cost of his services.

His business got off to a good start, but he knew there was a lot more potential within his existing client base.

I met with Paul to discuss the problem, and we arranged a workshop session to identify Lehrer & Feuerman's competitive advantages. We came up with six specific, critical competitive advantages:

- Lehrer & Feuerman represents only the corporate tenant/buyer, eliminating any possible conflict of interest. Over 97 percent of our competitors represent professional landlords, who control more than 75 percent of available properties in every submarket.

- Lehrer & Feuerman's average client saves a minimum of 30 percent on total occupancy and design construction costs. (We uncover and eliminate the hidden costs of every transaction and know which professionals have the skills to execute on time and within budget.)

- More than 80 percent of Lehrer & Feuerman's business is based on repeat clients, who have retained us for more than 350 transactions.

- Lehrer & Feuerman has advised more than 300 clients when *not* to sign a deal, due to a building's inefficiency (unusually high energy consumption, floor plate, elevator), deferred maintenance, ownership or property management, pending roadwork, abnormally high franchise fees charged on voice/data transmissions, and so on. We tell the truth even if it means "no sale."

- Lehrer & Feuerman principals are active participants

in transactions engaged. Our clients work directly with us, not with less experienced associates.

• Lehrer & Feuerman excels at executing complex transactions. (Case studies available.)

Once these competitive advantages were tested with existing and potential clients, and then given wide circulation, Lehrer & Feuerman began to see dramatic results. Two longtime, satisfied clients confessed that they didn't realize that Lehrer & Feuerman operated outside the Florida market and asked Lehrer & Feuerman to handle projects in North Carolina, Pennsylvania, Texas, and Louisiana. "We were engaged without the traditional beauty contest or a bake-off," Lehrer said.

In fact, prior and existing clients soon accounted for more than $3 million in expanded business, once they were made aware of all of Lehrer & Feuerman's competitive advantages. One client, who had been using Lehrer & Feuerman for seven years, brought in new business worth $1.5 million. Another, who hadn't used Lehrer & Feuerman in over twelve years, was so impressed by the competitive advantages that it brought Lehrer & Feuerman a new assignment—which took a mere sixty-three days to complete—that was worth another $1.6 million. Other referrals followed.

"I began to understand the value of articulating what made my new firm different from the masses," says Lehrer. He realized his two-person firm had distinct advantages over his competitors, even the publicly traded multinational with a team of thousands.

Lehrer now touts his competitive advantages to anyone who is interested, sometimes to great effect. "Flying to Hartford, Connecticut, I began a conversation with a stranger sitting across the aisle from me," recalls Lehrer. "Normally, when asked what I do for a living, I would give a thirty-second elevator commercial. Instead, I gave my competitive advantages."

His plane mate was so impressed, a deal was born soon after the plane landed. "Our first assignment for $13 million will close in the next ninety days, followed by $5 million and $20 million assignments." It can pay to replace your own elevator speech with competitive advantages.

THE HIGH COST OF NOT CLOSING

As the manager or owner of a business, it's awfully easy to assume that if your company is doing better than most of the competition, you're succeeding. But that kind of thinking invites the undertaker; for most businesses, it's grow or die. It doesn't matter how great your idea is; if it's underexploited, someone will steal it. Whatever your business, you have to establish yourself in the top tier in order to thrive. When GE's Jack Welch went on the biggest corporate buying spree in history in the 1980s and 1990s, he vowed that GE would never buy a business that ranked lower than third in its category. It also needed to have a very good chance of becoming number one. Welch was practicing what he preached: "If you don't have a competitive advantage, don't compete."

You must aim to be the most profitable company in your field, and you must come close to that goal. It's a matter of constant attention and adjustment. One of the gauges you should watch very closely to monitor your company's health is your rate of sales closings. It can tell you a lot about your business and what's wrong with it.

How much business are you losing because you don't close often enough? How much profit is lost? How much more profit would your company earn if you had a higher success rate on sales calls? According to one study in *Sales and Marketing* magazine, only 16 percent of all salespeople come within 90 percent of their quotas. How does your success rate compare?

How much would your own bottom line improve with higher closing rates? At the end of this chapter, you will find an exercise that will walk you through the math. (Or you can access the worksheet on my Web site, www. smartadvantage.com.)

WALL STREET LOVES COMPANIES WITH COMPETITIVE ADVANTAGES

The investment community is always on the lookout for companies with solid competitive advantages. Venture

capitalists, buyout firms, bankers, security analysts, brokers, and shrewd investors know what competitive advantage is all about. They seek out companies that have
clear-cut competitive advantages and know how to
exploit them. Warren Buffett, in an interview with Motley-
Fool.com, was asked what is the one thing to look for
when investing in a company. Without hesitation, he
replied, "Sustainable competitive advantage."

If you run a small, privately held company, bankers,
venture capitalists, and other investors will be a lot more
receptive to your financing needs. And if you ever decide
to sell or merge your company, your competitive advantages will bring a heftier selling price.

If you run a public company, your stock price will
reflect the value of your competitive advantages. Such
companies enjoy a premium on their share prices. In
fact, Morningstar, the financial ratings firm, closely
tracks what it calls the Bellwether 50 in its monthly
newsletter, *Morningstar StockInvestor*. It's a list of fifty
public companies that enjoy wide "economic moats"
around them to protect their core businesses from competitors. Mark Sellers, equities strategist at Morningstar,
assigns ratings that describe the size of the economic
moat each of the fifty companies enjoys. "Wide-moat
companies are those that have strong, sustainable
competitive advantages and high returns on capital," he
writes.

Sellers cites four characteristics of wide-moat companies:

- *Having high customer-switching costs.* Say your company uses Microsoft products, for example, and you want to switch to Apple. The cost of switching might be hard to justify.
- *Being the lowest-cost producer in a commodity market.* This is an enviable position to hold, but only a very few companies can claim that high ground.
- *Owning valuable intangible assets, such as patents and trademarks.*
- *Benefiting from the network effect.* The network effect, briefly, means that if you buy a product or service, your purchase indirectly benefits others who have bought the same product or service. Think cellular phones and computer software. The more the merrier.

Here is Morningstar's list of the top ten companies with "super-wide" moats around them. Sellers notes that only a handful of the more than 8,000 publicly traded companies that Morningstar tracks qualify for this elite status.

THE BELLWETHER TOP TEN

Wal-Mart. An obvious pick. Sellers notes that Wal-Mart can get away with charging 15 percent less for food than traditional supermarkets because of its superior buying power and distribution, and its lower labor costs.

Berkshire Hathaway. Among the many competitive advantages of this brainchild of Warren Buffett, Sellers cites the company's financial power, which gives it access to capital at lower costs than any other company in the universe. Having Buffett at the controls doesn't hurt, either.

Coca-Cola. Coke is a powerhouse because of its solid brands, marketing muscle, and global distribution. The company knows how to find new markets. "Our star is China," says Mary E. Minnick, who heads marketing, innovation, and growth strategy for the company. "We've had double-digit growth there over the last few years." Buffett's Berkshire Hathaway owns 200,000 shares of Coke, and Buffett sits on the company board.

Anheuser-Busch. Bud is the 2,000-pound gorilla in the beer industry and continues to improve its margins each year, Sellers notes. Mr. Competitive Advantage himself, Warren Buffett, bought a large block of Bud stock early in 2005. News of the purchase popped Bud stock 7 percent in a single day.

Wrigley. Quick. Name another brand of chewing gum. Stuck? No wonder. Wrigley's market share in the United States is over 50 percent. In parts of Europe, it's as high as 80 percent. Who can ever catch Wrigley?

Moody's. Sellers rates this investment-service company a "super-wide" for four reasons: high barriers to market entry; fat profit margins; low capital investment; solid growth prospects. Its management team is also shareholder-friendly.

Paychex. The company handles the payroll, human resource, and benefits chores for many of the nation's small-to-medium-sized businesses. Sellers points out that the business has low capital investment needs, and the cost of what it buys—data-processing equipment and software—tends to *decrease* over time. So margins grow even as the amount of business expands, a nice niche to be in.

Sysco. This $22.5-billion company distributes food and related products and services to restaurants, nursing homes, hospitals, hotels, motels, schools, colleges, cruise ships, sports parks, and summer camps—wherever a meal is prepared away from home. Sellers cites the company's "unparalleled" economies of scale in a fragmented industry.

eBay. Remember the "networking effect" we mentioned earlier? eBay's ace in the hole is this: The more sellers who use the online auction site, the more buyers they attract. And the more buyers there are, the more sellers they attract. No wonder it now has more than 60 million registered users, and counting.

Automatic Data Processing. What makes ADP so distinctive, according to Sellers, are its solid growth record, strong competitive positions in its markets, and a rock-solid balance sheet.

How do these top Bellwether stocks, distinguishable by their competitive advantages, fare against the market overall? Very well, thank you.

Morningstar states that its Bellwether 50 *gained* a total of 46.4 percent from July 31, 2000, through March 23, 2004, versus a *loss* of 19.5 percent for the Standard & Poor's 500 index. That's a difference of 66 percent. In dollar terms, that means the Bellwether portfolio, worth $100,000 on July 31, 2000, would have been worth $146,400 on March 23, 2004. A $100,000 portfolio invested in the S & P 500 would have been worth only $80,500 on that date.

Granted, this is a hypothetical assumption, since Morningstar didn't create the Bellwether 50 until 2001. But using a later time frame—from July 31, 2002, through March 23, 2004—the Bellwether 50 still outperformed the S & P 500, gaining 30.4 percent vs. 22.7 percent for the S & P. Does that mean you should run out and buy all the Bellwether 50 stocks and put your feet up?

Not really. Morningstar's Sellers says that blindly buying the highest-quality firms is not a good idea. (Just ask those who followed the "Nifty Fifty" strategy in the early 1970s.) "Instead, we highly recommend buying wide-moat companies if and only if their stocks are also selling at a compelling valuation." Even companies with super-wide moats can be overvalued at times. Morningstar keeps a watch list on the Bellwether 50 and alerts readers of its *StockInvestor* newsletter when they are favorably priced.

As Buffett himself puts it, "The key to investing is not assessing how much an industry is going to affect society, or how much it will grow, but rather determining the competitive advantage of any given company and, above all, the durability of that advantage."

It is interesting to note that most of the Bellwether 50 are not high-tech companies, by the way. The reason for this: It is very difficult for a company to hold on to a technological edge for long. How many times have you watched a red-hot company dissolve into thin air once the competition cranked out a copycat product or service? High-tech companies, especially start-ups, typically can't build much of a moat around themselves before the competition takes them on.

Most Bellwether companies are in mature, stable industries such as data processing, health care, and consumer products. They enjoy substantial internal competitive advantages that can take years, if not decades, to develop. Internal competitive advantages may not be visible to the customer, but he or she benefits from them nonetheless.

External competitive advantages—those the customer can see—can be developed a lot more quickly. Your company probably has some of them already, things like higher-quality goods, same-day delivery, three-hour service response time, and so on. Internal advantages include market position, buying power, economies of scale, government relations, and so on. Internal competitive advantages won't usually influence everyday customers, but they are very important to the company's financial health, its suppliers, bankers, stockholders, and employers. Throughout the rest of the book, we'll mainly focus on external competitive advantages.

INCREASE YOUR CLOSING RATE

How much business are you losing because would-be clients hesitate to sign on the dotted line? How much more profit would your company earn if you had a higher success rate on sales calls?

To help you figure out how much business your company leaves on the table, use this simple fill-in-the-blanks formula:

Your number of salespersons   _____
Multiply by average calls per week,
   per salesperson   _____
Equals total number of calls per week   _____

Current closing ratio   _____% = _____ deals per week
Should be   _____% = _____ deals per week
Difference   _____% = _____ deals per week
                                                     left on the table

Now ask yourself: What would it mean to your revenues if you could close an additional 10 percent of your deals just by providing a clear competitive advantage message? Here's one example: Let's say a medium-size company has 100 salespeople, making an average of 10 calls per week, for a total of 1,000 sales calls weekly. The current closing rate is 10 percent of calls. And the average deal is worth $600. Thus, the weekly gross is $60,000, or $3.12 million annually.

By increasing the closing rate to 20 percent, the annual gross doubles to $6.24 million. If the company had a profit margin of 35 percent on its products, its annual profit would jump from $1.09 million to $2.18 million just by increasing closing rates another 10 percent. Not only do annual profits double; the value of the company increases, too. If it's a public company, the stock will soar.

Once you have a handle on your own company's numbers, your have an excellent tool for gauging the effectiveness of your competitive advantage strategy. Let's assume that when you finish this book you will have a rock-solid list of quantifiable, unmatched competitive advantages. Let's also assume that your sales staff, employees, and anyone else who acts as an ambassador of your company has been indoctrinated with those competitive advantages. You've all begun promoting them every way you can.

After a few months, measure your sales closing rates again and compare them with a like period before you started touting your competitive advantages. If there isn't any improvement, then you need to go back to the drawing boards. You have not properly identified your competitive advantages. You must explore further how you can deliver something compelling that no one else has. (Market research can help.)

Remember, your competitive advantages are your deal closers. They are the reasons why your customers should do business with you rather than your competitors. And that is why companies with solid competitive advantages are worth so much more than those that lack them.

CHAPTER 3

Your Competitive Advantage Can Save Your Customers Money

It's Up to You to Show Them How

I OCCASIONALLY COACH SMALL AND MEDIUM-SIZE companies that have had a hard time winning big clients who often won't give them the time of day. Whatever the cause—corporate arrogance, lethargy, bureaucracy, or plain old habit—it is often difficult for a small-business owner to get the attention of a large corporation. How can smaller companies compete against larger, established suppliers? How can they sell their goods and services to large businesses when they don't have any visibility?

For many years McGraw-Hill, the publishing company, ran a corporate ad that has become an industry classic. It pictures a grumpy old CEO peering over his desk at a nervous young man who has come on a sales call. The crusty CEO says, "I don't know you, I don't know your products, I don't know your company. Now, what was it you wanted to talk to me about?"

McGraw-Hill's point was hardly subtle: Your salespeople will never get beyond the receptionist unless you increase your visibility by advertising in its business magazines. The subscribers to McGraw-Hill's publications are your potential customers, and advertising will get their attention.

There is no denying the value of advertising. But smaller companies lack the ad budgets to build extensive branding and awareness. Let's say you have a few specific sales targets in mind, where advertising isn't appropriate. If you are after a few big fish, and need the right bait, try money. No matter how indifferent the corporate whales may seem, if you can save them money, they'll be interested—provided you can prove it. If you can, you have one dynamite competitive advantage in your bait bucket.

One of my favorite examples of the small boat catching the whale involves H. B. Trim, a niche supplier in the garment industry, providing buttons, zippers, lining and hangars, plastic garment bags, and other trim materials to large apparel makers throughout the Western Hemisphere. As the manufacturers send the unfinished fabrics to, say, Guatemala, to be sewn into garments, H. B. Trim provides them with the trim needed to finish the garments before shipping them to retailers in the United States. It's a business where margins are thinner than the plastic sheets in which the clothes are wrapped.

The owner of the company, Ross Nadelman, was a client of mine. Ross cut his teeth in the garment industry working for his brother's company in New York. When the company shifted production to Miami, Ross packed his bags and headed for the Sunshine State. After five years, he tired of running production and (with his brother's blessings) started his own company. When he contacted me, his business was doing well enough, but Ross wasn't satisfied. He understood the essence of competitive advantage and viewed his business as a "work in progress."

I met with him at a local coffee shop, over fried eggs and home fries, to discuss his company's revenue growth, which appeared to be stalling. Somewhat animated, he leaned over close to my face and said, "I do everything better than my competition. I offer more. I understand the business more, and I can deliver better." I'd never met an entrepreneur more passionate about what he had to offer his potential customers.

Yet much of his potential market wasn't getting it. His message wasn't strong enough and certainly wasn't loud enough. "There are two companies in New York that I need to get into," he said. "I have been tapping on the door for years, and they won't give me the time of day. I can save them so much time and money, if I could just get them to understand."

"Okay," I said. "What would you say to them if you did get in front of them?"

He looked at me and scowled, "I can't get in front of them! That's the problem!"

"Let's say you do get to see them," I persisted. "Pretend I am their decision maker and you have my attention. What are you going to say?"

Without blinking, he said, "I can save you a lot of time and money—just give me the chance."

Getting into my role as a tough prospective buyer, I told him it wasn't good enough. Every vendor has that same line. "How can you do it and how much money are we talking about?" I asked.

Ross was quick with the "how." Both of the companies that he had been pursuing for years took care of their trim needs themselves. They bought, stored, and shipped the trim to factories abroad, where their garments are sewn and finished. They were convinced such vertical integration was the cheapest way to go. But Ross could save them the time, trouble, labor, and expense of maintaining extensive inventory of trim items, warehousing, freight, and bilingual documentation. From his own awareness of the industry, he knew that they were spending way too much on their trim operations. He could provide one-stop shopping at a significant cost savings.

I then asked him to get specific. "Exactly how much money can you save Leslie Fay?" (That company was one of his major targets.) He shrugged, looking a little like a kid who doesn't have the answer the teacher wants. He whispered, "How could I know what they spend? I don't have access to that information."

"But *they* know what those costs are," I said. "They don't have to tell *you* what they are. As long as you can do the same job for a lot less, it is a case of simple math for them to figure out how much they can save."

We drafted a letter to Ross's contact at Leslie Faye and included a little note and worksheet:

> Clearly, I don't know what you spend annually on each of these overhead items, but I can significantly reduce these costs for you: Would you please take a moment and fill in these line items to total the savings you would have if we handled your trim?
>
> | | |
> |---|---|
> | Inventory | $_____ |
> | Documentation administration | $_____ |
> | Employee overhead | $_____ |
> | Administration expense | $_____ |
> | Storage/warehouse expense | $_____ |
> | Your total savings if we handle your trim business | $_____ |

We also included in the letter a list of the competitive advantages that H. B. Trim offers over other trim businesses:

- The largest U.S/Central American/Caribbean inventory available, meeting all of your needs.
- Twice as many employees as our competition, special-

izing in both production as well as trim, to more efficiently serve you.

- The possibility of using our warehouse as your own warehousing facility, thus eliminating storage and consolidation overhead.
- Bilingual documentation fully handled by our staff, eliminating or minimizing your administrative overhead.
- Savings of $250,000 to $350,000 on freight per year, as we will ship your partial shipments on our containers when space is available.

We were so anxious for the client to see the letter that we decided to send it by e-mail. Ross knew exactly who should get it—he had been trying to see her for years. We didn't have to wait long for a response. Within two hours, Ross got a phone call from the would-be client, who invited him to come to New York in a few days. Within two weeks he landed the account, which netted his company $1 million in the first year alone.

Ross was so excited with the results that he sent a similar letter to a second prospect, using the same bait. It worked again. This time it landed him $2 million in new business. And all he did was ask his clients to take a moment to figure out the true savings they would realize by using his firm. Since applying this technique, Ross says his business has increased 60 percent. (Leslie Faye later collapsed into bankruptcy, and I've often wondered if that would have happened had its management heeded the Ross Nadelmans of the world earlier.)

WE SAVED THEM MONEY—
WHY NOT YOU?

When it comes to saving your clients money, the more specific you can be, the louder your message will sound. Seitlin Human Resources saves its clients money and a lot of potential headaches by taking care of all their human resource needs—firing, hiring, compliance, administration, and so on. But it can be tough to persuade a potential client that those touted savings are real. Again, the refrain "We can save you money" simply doesn't register with buyers. No one believes it anymore. It's necessary to prove it.

Dr. Jack Mitchell, the president of Seitlin HR, attended one of my seminars and later asked me to work with him to make his competitive advantages believable to more clients. So we decided to get specific. We'd tell them exactly how much they could anticipate saving, based on Seitlin's experience with other companies. These are the competitive advantages and positioning statements that were finally hammered out for his target market of companies with twenty-five or more employees:

- We save client companies $30K to $50K annually in human resource management costs.
- We reduce client companies' turnover rate by a minimum of 10 percent, saving companies $100K-plus annually. (We help retain good employees.)

- We help clients achieve zero lawsuits against them for wrongful terminations, discrimination, or sexual harassment.
- We maintain a 97 percent client retention rate.

Those are powerful statements, and they've won Seitlin many more clients.

RELIABILITY AND QUALITY CAN SAVE YOUR CLIENTS MONEY

Sometimes you save your clients money without their realizing it. So tell them. One client of mine runs a company that repairs and services office equipment. He found himself facing heavy price competition. While he could offer a lot of intangibles as competitive advantages—his repair service record was better, his guarantees covered more, and his equipment was more reliable than his competitor's—he didn't know what this meant to the customer in terms of dollars and cents. The CEO couldn't know for sure, so he asked potential customers to fill in the numbers themselves. How many hours of downtime did they experience on their office machines in the last year? What was the hourly cost of that downtime? By simple multiplication, they could easily quantify the dollars spent—and my client's competitive advantage. His fast repairs and superior equipment meant there was virtually no downtime.

Determining your competitive advantage could involve finding a way to quantify quality. A seafood supplier contacted me when he noticed that his company was losing market share in his smoked salmon division. The reason was price. Because his competitor was a start-up and didn't have the overhead my client had, price became the differentiator, and my guy was losing. After I met with the CEO and discussed the problem, we did a workshop with his salespeople.

It emerged that, unlike his competitors, my client smoked his salmon every day, just prior to delivery. So his customers—mainly food markets and delis—always received fresh product, no matter what day the salmon was delivered. It had a longer shelf life than competitors' salmon, which could already be days out of the smoker by the time it was delivered, and therefore spoiled faster.

The supermarkets and delis could sell more of my client's freshly smoked salmon before it spoiled. The longer shelf life meant more cash in the register for every pound of salmon bought. That is a decided competitive advantage. The sales team went to work quantifying this to customers, and the competition faded.

CUSTOMERS WILL PAY MORE TO GET MORE

You're doubtless familiar with the term "value added." Much has been written about the concept, but the term pretty much defines itself—getting something for nothing, or practically nothing—an automatic add-on. What extras do you provide your customers, above and beyond the basic product or service you provide? These value-added items can save your customers a lot of money, headaches, and time, and if your competition doesn't provide them, voilà! You have an important competitive advantage to tell your customers about.

When I make presentations before CEO groups, I am always amazed at how infrequently companies take credit for all the value added they provide. If you offer something your competitors don't, make sure your customers know about it. It is another marketing arrow in your quiver.

Anyone who travels a lot, as I do, knows that renting a car at the airport is pretty much a matter of pick 'em. Step up to the car-rental platform and you can rent the same car, at almost the same price, from three or more on-site car-rental companies. All offer discounts and frequent-user rewards, special check-in privileges for valued customers, and so on. It could be hard to find a competitive advantage at the airport car-rental counter. No wonder Avis got extra mileage from its meaningless slogan "We try harder." Any differentiation was seen as a plus, even one as vague as Avis's.

But that was before Hertz decided to go the extra mile. And am I glad that Hertz did. A few years ago, the giant firm—still No. 1, and now being sold by Ford—decided to add global positioning systems in some of its cars. These marvelous devices, supplied with data from satellites somewhere in the heavens, tell you exactly where you are at all times.

I accept that I am directionally challenged (no sexist comments, please). So when out of town on unfamiliar turf, I always use Hertz. The Hertz system, called Never-Lost, is familiar to new-car owners with the OnStar GPS system. You tap in your destination and a street map appears on the screen, showing your best route outlined in purple, how far away it is, and how long it should take to get there. As you drive, the map indicates your progress in real time. But you never have to take your eyes off the road—the system talks to you. "Turn left on Green Street, a half-mile away." A few seconds before you are due to turn, a chime goes off as a reminder.

The first time I used it, I was traveling to give a seminar in northern New Jersey, an area of the world infamous for its maddening road signage. Some of the signs are counterintuitive (you make a right to find a hidden jug-handle that takes you left, for example). Or the signs are posted too close to the exits, so you can easily breeze by before noticing them. Others are obscured, hard to read at night, or simply not where they should be. I've missed more than one flight trying to find my way back from the wilds of suburban New Jersey to Newark Airport.

Because of this, I was an instant convert to Hertz, which has far more onboard navigation systems than the competition. NeverLost has saved me from being late to appointments and has gotten me safely back to airports all over the country with no fumbling for maps, no stops at gas stations, no anxiety about having missed a critical turn. I cannot quantify how much the Hertz system has saved me in dollars, but how do you put a price tag on not getting lost? Not being late? Not missing flights? Not having to stress over finding the new client, or the conference center where I am the guest speaker?

The cost for the NeverLost system is about $9 a day in addition to the rental charge. That's a small price to pay for the peace of mind it brings and the time it saves. (Of course, if Sherman McCoy, the protagonist in Tom Wolfe's classic *Bonfire of the Vanities,* had a NeverLost system on board his Mercedes, the book would have lost its plot.)

What is surprising is that only Hertz makes this onboard system widely available. Nationally, some 50,000 Hertz cars were equipped with NeverLost by 2004, and 10,000 more were added in 2005. Some competitors now offer portable, plug-in navigation systems. But they are awkward to use compared to the user-friendly NeverLost. For customers like myself, and I'm sure there are plenty of us, the feature has become a necessity. Which means I always use Hertz. Why don't the competitors get wise and install similar systems? They eventually must, of course. Remember, most competitive advantages have a limited life span. But meantime, Hertz has put me—and a lot of other frequent flyers—in the driver's seat. I am hooked on NeverLost, and as a result, I love Hertz: exactly what you want your company's competitive advantages to mean to your customer.

One Hertz competitor told a journalist that his rental company lacked such systems in its cars because there was not much customer demand for them. Reflect on that a bit: The customers who *do* demand them are on the Hertz line. When researching your customers, you should always include the ones who got away. By the way, Hertz reported record earnings in 2004.

DELIVERING "THE RIGHT STUFF"

Your customers, or would-be customers, need to be informed and reminded of what added values you provide them—extras that can save them money, time, and aggravation. Yet too many business owners and managers can be ignorant of what those competitive advantages are. The seafood supplier didn't communicate that he was selling fresher salmon with longer shelf life, and thus enhancing his customers' bottom lines, until a competitor threatened his market share.

You could be providing a lot of extras to your customers without realizing how much you are actually saving them. Or, if you do not provide meaningful extras now, you might consider adopting them. They can be critical competitive advantages. Consider the following:

Terms. If you are a small or medium-size company up against a category killer, you might have flexible financing terms that the big guys can't match. For example, a lumber company in the Northeast enjoyed a robust business with little substantial competition until Home Depot began to close in. One Home Depot box opened twenty miles away, and then another just ten miles down the road. Observers predicted that the lumber company would soon be bulldozed out of business.

Surely, it couldn't compete on price, not against Home Depot's buying power. Lumber is lumber. So it concentrated on hitting Home Depot where it was vulnerable. It offered more-flexible credit arrangements for its most important customers—small contractors who often lack lines of credit from banks. The lumber company didn't have to drop its prices to stay in business. It adopted new competitive advantages.

Guarantees. It is common for attendees at my seminars to tell me that their companies are "the only ones in our industry offering multiyear guarantees" on their products. But when I ask if they make a big deal about the guarantee to prospective buyers, most admit they do not.

The reason is usually the same: "If we emphasize the guarantee, too many customers may take advantage of it."

That's a pretty lame excuse. Either you offer a guarantee or you don't. If you are confident enough in the product to guarantee it in the first place, make a selling point of it. Statistics show that a very small percentage of customers in any business actually use the guarantee. But the guarantee takes a lot of risk out of the buying decision and clinches a lot of deals.

Inventory turns. One of my favorite stories about inventory turns involves a clothing manufacturer who sold women's clothes to boutiques around the country. When I asked him what differentiated him from his competitors, he said he thought his clothes were "wearable."

"As opposed to what?" I asked, trying not to laugh. He began to talk about design, fabric, cut, and so on. When I queried what his competitors were saying, he shrugged and said, "I suppose the same thing . . . but I know my stuff sells much better."

I asked him what his customer, the boutique owner, cares about most. "Whether or not it sells," he said. So I asked if his shop owners measured inventory turns. He answered that some did, some did not. I suggested that he teach them how to measure inventory turns and then he could prove to the shop owners his clothes sold better.

My point was that he should stop selling "wearable clothes" like everyone else and start selling inventory turns. Moving the goods is what matters.

Note: Be sure you can back up your boast. Your buyers will know soon enough if you can't. As with any competitive advantage you claim, make sure you deliver.

Materials. One client in the home-improvement business who sold siding knew his product was "stronger and better" because of the materials he used. But he didn't know how to convey that without sounding biased and subjective. Upon asking his employees a series of questions, I learned from one of his engineers that the company's product has a higher wind load rating than any competitive product. In many geographic markets, the higher load rating influences buying decisions. So if your materials are stronger and provide customers with a benefit, shout about it in a way that is measurable.

Delivery. If you provide the same product as your competitors but you offer better delivery service, you have a competitive advantage. But how important is it? The Compleat Company, which sells promotional products, decided to find out. The Seattle-based company polled its customers about the importance of its on-time delivery. It found that its customers not only valued that service highly, they had a pretty low tolerance for being late.

Eighty-eight percent of its customers defined "on-time delivery" as being on schedule 97 percent of the time or better. Only 4 percent of its customers would accept an on-schedule rate of less than 93 percent. A manager from Compleat told me that the company is now focusing its energy and resources to make sure it meets that expectation. When Compleat's customers want their deliveries, they will get them.

Information. In business, as in war, intelligence can be priceless. In *Business @ the Speed of Thought* (Warner, 1999), Bill Gates writes: "The most meaningful way to differentiate your company from your competition, the best way to put distance between you and the crowd, is to do an outstanding job with information. How you gather, manage, and use information will determine whether you win or lose."

Knowing what your competitors are doing, and keeping up with trends in your industry, are basic forms of intelligence, and essential if you are going to run a successful business. So is listening to your customers. (Your own and your competitors'.)

The more competitive the business you are in, the more important the role of intelligence. You can't afford to get caught flatfooted if, say, a labor strike shuts off deliveries of critically needed material. Or if commodity prices suddenly spike or drop. Or consumer confidence sinks. Or if new products being developed by your competitors threaten your markets.

No matter what business you are in, failing to keep a weather eye on changes in your industry can be fatal. A lot of this "intelligence" is hardly proprietary. It simply amounts to smart business practices born out of experience. If you are a B-to-B supplier who sells to retailers, your customers' success determines how well you do, too. Your experience can help your clients avoid common mistakes.

Small and medium-size businesses are often in the dark about key developments in their industries. They lack the time, money, and expertise to gather and evaluate that information. But that doesn't mean it isn't important. Consider the prices they pay for the goods or services they buy. Advance word of radical price shifts, or new products that will make others obsolete, can save them from missing a buying opportunity, or from laying in inventory that will soon become obsolete.

Keeping your customers informed of trends can only make them healthier, and in turn create more business for you. Word of mouth from your sales force is one time-honored way to accomplish this. But in this age of the Internet there are other effective ways, too, from e-mail to Web sites that keep clients posted on prices and other industry developments.

One of my former clients, the Institute for Trend Research, in Concord, New Hampshire, analyzes market and economic trends and makes accurate predictions as to when those trends will change. Its business is its forecasting expertise in a wide range of sectors, from industrial construction and agricultural market movement to interest rates, commodity prices, and inflation.

Subscribers to the company's publication *EcoTrends* get an important bonus: a discount on EcoCharts. EcoCharts, using raw data that the subscribers provide themselves, tells them which indicators included in *EcoTrends* correlate best to their specific businesses. ITR has defined four phases of economic movement; if the trends that affect your industry are in Phase C, then you are expecting a downturn. Your actions might include a reduction in inventory and training, an avoidance of long-term purchase commitments, and deeper concentration on your cash and balance sheet. On the other hand, during Phase B, an upward trend, you would accelerate training, increase prices, consider outside manufacturing, and open distribution centers. This kind of information can provide companies with powerful competitive advantages.

Training. Many large companies offer specialized training for their customers, free or at cost, so they can run their business better. McDonald's runs its own academy for new franchise owners, for example, so they can learn to avoid common pitfalls and maximize the return on their investments. The company draws on the experiences of thousands of other franchise owners and shares that knowledge, because it is vital to their own business. I often recommend to clients that if they invest heavily in training they should make a competitive point of it. For example, "We invest half a million dollars each year training our employees" or ". . . training our customers."

NOTHING CHEESY ABOUT IT

MCT Dairies, Inc., is a wholesale supplier of quality cheese and dairy products. It offers dairy products at factory-direct prices in less-than-truckload quantities. Since it is essentially a commodity business and price competition is fierce, it puts a lot of emphasis on customer satisfaction.

In looking for a competitive advantage over its competitors, MCT found that its customers were starved for pricing data and other news and information about the dairy industry—information that MCT had at its fingertips.

So the company started a Web site for its customers and periodically publishes an online newsletter for them. It reports and discusses commodities pricing of dairy products, the latest news from the U.S. Dept of Agriculture, and other issues important to the industry. Customers love it. The newsletter has built loyalty and attracted new business, because the information supplied saves their customers money by letting them know the best time to buy.

SHOW CUSTOMERS HOW MUCH
YOU SAVE THEM

Nothing grabs the attention of prospective customers quicker than showing them how much money, time, and effort they can save by doing business with you. But it's up to you to quantify those savings.

Make a list of your actions/products/services that make your customers' job easier and more profitable. Perhaps you provide free employee training. Or maybe your products are more reliable and have fewer defects. Maybe you deliver more often, or at more convenient hours. Maybe your packaging allows for easier handling and reduces damage. Maybe you reduce your customers' warehousing costs by offering frequent deliveries in various quantities.

Make estimates of how much money your customers and prospects save by using your product or service versus the competition. Show them in dollars and cents wherever possible. If you can't pinpoint those costs, ask the customers themselves to come up with their own numbers, as H. B. Trim did. When the customer crunches the numbers himself, he is a lot easier to convince.

If you can't get numbers from the customer, report how much money you saved similar clients. The more specific you can be, the better.

Talk to your customers and prospects about their business problems. It's important to understand your customers' businesses, perhaps even better than they do themselves. If you learn, as The Compleat Company did, that on-time delivery has high significance to your customers, then it should be your mission to create measurements and a culture that will support it.

Don't assume your existing customers know all the benefits you are providing them. What are you doing for them that they take for granted? What would it cost them otherwise? Remember, it is far more expensive to gain a new customer than to retain a valued one.

CHAPTER 4

Competitive Advantages Free You from Price-Based Competition

THOUGH SPOKEN WELL BEFORE MY TIME, BASEBALL legend Satchel Paige's famous line, "Don't look back, someone may be gaining on you," lives on. Good advice for an aging baseball pitcher, but it won't help someone running a business. The better your business is, the more competitors you are likely to have. Succeed, and they will come, and you can't afford to ignore them. That's why it pays to stay up to speed on your competitive advantages. They are your armor and your weapons. It makes no sense to wait for your competitors to start chipping away at your business before you make the most of them. You may be too late.

Clients often approach me *after* they have lost business to their competitors—which is hardly the best time to identify, research, and broadcast your competitive advantages to your customers. The entire process usually takes several months (although my clients and I have done it a lot faster in emergency cases).

In my experience, most business owners and managers threatened by the competition have the same look about them: one not of depression or defeat, but of determination to fight. That's a healthy response, but why get yourself in such a pickle in the first place? The result of a dogfight with a major competitor or competitors is all too often a price war, a battle usually won by the guy with the deepest pockets. You have to provide your customers with more than the lowest price. And the sooner you can identify and promote your competitive advantages—or develop and implement new ones—the better positioned you'll be to fend off competitors.

When you promote your competitive advantages and identify new ones, you are making preemptive strikes against competitors who rely strictly on price. Let the other guy go broke with the price strategy, and never get down in the mud to wrestle with someone who outweighs you.

A client in the health care industry arranged for one of my workshops at what turned out to be a very critical time for his company. His company manages and operates hospital emergency rooms, providing everything from doctors and nurses to billing. It is a rapidly growing field—and has attracted a lot of players. My client, who operates in the Northeast region, kept an eye on the competition and thought he was keeping them at bay.

On the very morning of the workshop, however, a crisis arose. His biggest customer had just informed him that he was thinking of switching to a lower-cost competitor. The CEO was calm and gracious as he excused himself from the workshop to drive over and see that customer. A very large chunk of his business was suddenly at stake.

A cloud hung over the room for the next few hours. While the management team went through exercises to arrive at competitive advantages, the CEO was trying to keep the company's biggest customer. I couldn't help thinking that if the CEO had put his managers through the workshop a few months earlier, he might not have had to make that emergency visit. His customer would have already been provided with a list of persuasive competitive advantages to offset the competitor's lowball pitch.

When the CEO returned to the workshop about noon, he was all smiles. He informed his troops that the customer wasn't going anywhere. The cloud dissipated, and the CEO took a chair and eagerly joined in the exercises. He didn't need any more convincing of the importance of competitive advantages when you're faced with a low-balling competitor. To keep the customer, he had to come up with a very impressive competitive advantage on the spot, but it cost him. He agreed to run that hospital's operation personally for the next year, which meant he had to spend a lot more time on one customer than he would have liked.

After the workshop session and customer research, the CEO could articulate exactly what his competitive advantages were. Key among them was the level of patient satisfaction, which ranked in the industry's top tier. Another was the number of board-certified physicians on staff. No longer would he have to make the kind of costly under-pressure promise he had to commit to on the spot to keep his biggest customer.

Without a competitive advantage, price becomes your only differentiator. When all the customer has to go on is cost, it's easy for him to perceive you as the same as the competition. And that leads to margin erosion. When you're seen as a commodity supplier rather than a marketer, your margins will begin to shrink, and inevitably, you'll be absorbed or go out of business. Why should a customer choose to do business with you when he thinks he is getting a better deal somewhere else for the same product or service?

HOW TO TACKLE WAL-MART

If a competitor is bigger and richer than you are, you'll never beat him on price. He can buy cheaper than you can, because he buys in much higher volume and has purchasing muscle with suppliers. So his margins are better even if you both charge the same prices. There are other economies of scale you can't match. For example, Wal-Mart's inventory control is one of its less-visible, internal competitive advantages that is the envy of most competitors.

Wal-Mart has enjoyed extraordinary success since Sam Walton opened his first store in Rogers, Arkansas, in 1962. It is the world's biggest retailer, with revenues that topped $285 billion in 2004. It has more than 1.5 million employees, and over 5,200 stores around the globe, including 550 Sam's Club outlets. Three out of every four Americans live within a fifteen-minute drive of a Wal-Mart. Nearly three-quarters of its stores are in the United States, but Wal-Mart is expanding rapidly in Asia, Europe, and South America and is already the largest retailer in Canada and Mexico.

Along the way, Wal-Mart has crushed thousands of small retailers and dozens of large ones, including giants like Bradlees, Caldor, Circuit City, Toys "R" Us, and Winn-Dixie. Wal-Mart beat them all on price, pure and simple. But that didn't stop Kmart, which had long suffered in Wal-Mart's widening shadow, from waging a price war. In 2001, Kmart hit upon what it thought was a brilliant strategy that would win customers away from its archrival. It would undersell Wal-Mart on popular household products, which it touted in its daily "Blue-Light Specials." The rationale was that customers in search of the specials would do additional shopping at the store, making up for the items that were being sold at or below cost. Or so went the theory.

For a while, the strategy appeared to be working. Sales volume increased. But profit margins shrank faster than cheap T-shirts. Shoppers snapped up the loss-leader items on sale at Kmart but still shopped at competitors like Wal-Mart for other items. Profits vanished, and Kmart filed for Chapter 11. Dozens of stores were closed, thousands of workers were fired, and investors lost billions. Kmart eventually merged with Sears to form Sears Holdings Corporation, which so far has had little success in returning Kmart to its former glory. The chain continues to close stores and lay off workers.

But as big and strong and smart as it is, Wal-Mart can be had. To paraphrase Lincoln, it can't sell all the people all they want all the time. There is still plenty of room for competition. In a report called "Outsmarting Wal-Mart" (*Harvard Business Review,* December 2004), Darrell Digby and Dan Hass cite big retailers that are doing very well despite the ubiquity of Wal-Mart. The authors, analysts at Bain & Co., cited the following:

Best Buy. The chain has a larger assortment and better-quality electronic products than Wal-Mart. "Additionally, the company differentiates itself from Wal-Mart by the services it provides to its customers, such as its in-house repair team called the 'Geek Squad,'" note Digby and Hass. If you've ever had to return something to Best Buy, you know it's almost a pleasure. No hassle, no questions asked. And if you have to wait for, say, your computer to be programmed while you are there, you'll be given a beeper device to let you know when it's ready (courtesy of the folks at JTECH, the company I described in Chapter 2).

Target. The retailer has successfully differentiated itself by selling trendy, designer clothing and home products that are a grade above Wal-Mart's merchandise. The layout and design of the stores are more attractive, too.

Walgreens. The pharmacy chain has more brands and a wider assortment of drug and cosmetic products, and its stores are open 24/7.

PetsMart. The specialized chain offers a wider variety of pet products than Wal-Mart, offers grooming services, has knowledgeable staff, and also allows customers to bring their pets into the stores.

Digby and Hass also cite two privately held retail food chains that do more than hold their own against Wal-Mart—HEB and Publix. Again, they succeed because of the variety and quality of the foods they sell, not because they have the lowest prices.

Matthew Meier, writing in *Business 2.0* (May 2005), published his own take on "How to Beat Wal-Mart." He came up with four other companies that not only have thrived in Wal-Mart's shadow, but also have benefited directly from what Wal-Mart has created.

Costco. Even though the warehouse club has 218 fewer outlets than archrival Sam's Club, in 2004 Costco had $47 billion in sales and $882 million in profits. The Wal-Mart unit reported $37 billion in sales and an estimated profit of only

$200 million. The secret? Selling high-end products (such as Dom Perignon, Cartier watches, Waterford crystal, Godiva chocolates) at deep discounts to status-hungry small-business owners. Costco found that small-business owners are often the wealthiest people in the community but are also typically stingy. They want status products, but at bargain prices. Costco's buying power allows it to discount the luxury goods that pull in those targeted customers.

Dollar Tree. With nothing on its shelves priced at over $1, the discount chain now has 2,735 locations and revenues of $3.2 billion. You'll find odd lots, remainders, and discounted, no-name merchandise at Dollar Tree stores. You'll also often find smaller-size versions of brand-name products, priced to sell at $1 or under. The stores sell an eighteen-ounce bottle of Dawn dishwashing soap, for example, which contains two ounces less than the standard size. Customers love it. Procter & Gamble, Dial, and Clorox have begun to develop special products for Dollar Tree, for two reasons: The stores move an ever-growing amount of product, which, in turn, gives the manufacturers a bit of leverage against Wal-Mart's buying power.

Dollar Tree aims directly at Wal-Mart customers and locates its stores close to Wal-Marts. About half are within two miles of the "category killer's" stores.

Save-A-Lot. The $4 billion grocery-store chain flies under Wal-Mart's radar by placing its stores in less affluent neighborhoods—those where family incomes are below

$35,000 a year. These are traditionally underserved markets. Save-A-Lot's 1,250 outlets in 39 states are relatively small, with 20 or so employees and only 1,250 or so items on the shelves. (Wal-Mart supercenters have up to 40,000 items available.) There is usually only a single brand of each item, often bearing a private label. By keeping the inventory limited, Save-A-Lot's warehouses can deliver a branch's entire order on a single truck. The result: Save-A-Lot's prices can be as much as 15 percent below those of Wal-Mart. Yet the chain has a higher profit margin—3.5 percent—against Wal-Mart's 2.6 percent margin on groceries.

Dick's Sporting Goods. While Wal-Mart sells more sports equipment than anyone else (about $6 billion annually), Dick's is now the second-largest sporting goods retailer in the nation, with annual sales of over $2 billion and a yearly growth rate averaging 20 percent. Its competitive advantages: Dick's offers an excellent variety, and it coddles the customer. If you're looking for golf equipment, you'll get advice from a real pro. Some 200 PGA pros work at Dick's in-store golf shops. Exercise equipment? They have personal trainers in most stores. Hunting or fishing gear? Tennis equipment? You'll find resident experts to advise you. You can even test out equipment on the premises. There are golf cages with computer-simulated golf courses, and indoor running tracks to try out new sneakers. You can also have your tennis racket restrung or your bicycle fixed on the premises.

TAKE A LOOK AROUND
THE NEIGHBORHOOD

There is evidence all around you of how businesses can thrive without competing on price. And those businesses have this in common: They offer something that is more important to the consumer than the lowest possible price.

I like an occasional glass of wine at dinner, and I'm frugal. I buy 1.5-liter bottles of Ruffino Chianti, a pleasant red that stays good for a few days after it's uncorked. A single bottle can last through a few meals.

At the three retailers in my neighborhood, the price of the Chianti ranges from $11.99 to $20.49. Same wine, same year, same-size bottle. Why on earth would anyone shop at the store selling the most expensive bottle? While you mull that over, I'll add this clue: I usually go to the store with the cheapest price—but not always.

The answer is convenience. The first wine retailer is the local supermarket, where I routinely do my food shopping. Another is a store a few blocks away, within walking distance from my home—and he delivers. The third is an off-the-beaten-path discount liquor store that is fifteen minutes away by car. I go to the discounter when time allows and buy a case (he doesn't deliver). When that runs out, I'll buy at the supermarket or the nearby store until I can spare the time to get to the discounter.

All three stores seem to be doing very well, thank you. But I worry about the discounter, as Internet wine sales become legal in my state. The discounter can still compete on price for now, as the cheapest online price I could find for the wine was $11.99, plus shipping. But if I were in his shoes, I'd get a delivery truck and arrange for free drop-offs in the evenings. That would be his competitive advantage against the Internet retailer. Bear in mind that:

- Customers will spend more for convenience. If you can save them time, energy, aggravation, or uncertainty, even if you're not the lowest-cost seller, you will succeed (Best Buy, Save-A-Lot, Walgreens).
- Customers will also pay more for higher quality and trendier products (Target).
- Customers will pay more for expert advice and personal service (Dick's Sporting Goods, PetsMart).
- Customers will pay more for image—their own, not yours. Seiko watches are as reliable as Cartier, but they lack the cachet. If you sell luxury goods at discount, customers will come (Costco).
- Customers always love a perceived bargain with a broad assortment (Dollar Tree, Costco).

THE CATEGORY KILLER
IN YOUR BAILIWICK

Retailing is not the only field in which category killers like Wal-Mart roam. There are giants in virtually every business you can name—from accounting (the Big Four) and advertising (Interpublic) to publishing (Random House) and real estate (Coldwell Banker), from financial services (Fidelity) and banking (Citigroup) to media and entertainment (Fox).

The list goes on. Chances are, if you're in business, you have a category killer or two to worry about. But don't take your eye off your other competitors, either. In the *Harvard Business Review* report cited above, the authors quote the CEO of a Wal-Mart competitor: "It's like the two outdoorsmen who wake to find a raging bear at their campsite. One camper stands and slowly backs away; the other starts to lace up his sneakers. 'You can't outrun the bear!' whispers the first. 'I don't have to,' replies the second. 'I just have to outrun you!'"

You know the bear is out there. If he comes after you, remember that the most important thing is to outrun the other camper first. The bear is going to eat. But you don't want to be the meal.

SIZE HAS ITS DRAWBACKS, TOO

Like bears, category killers aren't inevitable victors. Sometimes they get so hungry they go berserk. Consider Enron. It controlled huge chunks of the gas and electricity markets in the United States, and even built a nuclear plant in India, but it couldn't resist grasping for more markets. It made an attempt to be the world's largest water company. And it tried to corner the market on broadband capacity. Enron lost billions on these ventures, started cooking the books, and the rest is history. Sometimes the category killer will cannibalize itself.

Or take Clear Channel Communications, the radio giant, and its foray into the pop concert business. Why make such an expansion? It already owned dozens of concert venues and played the music of rock stars all the time on its hundreds of radio stations. Think of all that synergy!

In 2000, Clear Channel paid $4.5 billion for concert promoter SFX and went to work promoting concerts, using bigger-name stars (with bigger salaries) playing at bigger venues (at higher cost). But instead of packed houses, performers stared out at a lot of empty seats. Ticket prices were just too high for large audiences. Clear Channel lost a fortune before deciding to spin off Clear Channel Music Group as a separate company. Sometimes category killers get blinded by their own hype.

And sometimes they can be victims of their own success. In their early years, the stock of category killers often skyrockets long before real profits merit such high prices. But once the low-hanging fruit is plucked, future growth comes with higher costs. Margins slip. Stockholders start screaming. CEOs sometimes will do crazy things to get the stockholders off their back (not to mention greatly increase the value of their own stock options). WorldCom and Enron cooked the books. Time-Warner

CEO Jerry Levin engineered the boneheaded sellout to AOL, paid for with hideously overpriced stock.

Category killers stumble and sometimes fall. You can learn to live with them and even beat them.

ONE SIZE DOESN'T FIT ALL

Howard F. Wasserman was in fine fettle when he arrived with his management team for one of my workshops on competitive advantage. He promptly donned a pair of those oversize, gag sunglasses and began hamming it up. (We hand out little toys at the beginning of our workshops, to loosen things up.)

Wasserman, CEO of Nailite International, a maker of siding products, rates as one of the funniest CEOs I've ever dealt with, and he was quick with the gags all morning. But he is serious about his business. While jokes about siding salesmen have been around for decades— recall Danny DeVito in *The Tin Men*—there is nothing funny about shoddy siding.

Of course, there are different kinds of siding, in different materials with different characteristics, textures, and colors. Despite the old, shady image, siding is a booming industry, fueled by the record pace of new home and commercial construction and renovation. Nailite's siding is not the inexpensive vinyl stuff you buy by the yard at home-improvement stores. Its molded plastic panels undergo a proprietary coating process and are more than twice the thickness of vinyl. Nailite's replica cedar, brick, and stone siding looks just like the real McCoy but holds up much better against the elements. The product is also less costly than the real thing but is more durable and attractive, and it is easier to maintain. The company has been in business for over twenty-five years, but it now faces more competition than ever, from companies small and large—including giants Alcoa and CertainTeed.

When we convened to identify Nailite's competitive advantages, I had my doubts about the company coming up with any dramatic new findings. Wasserman is a very savvy manager who was already thriving in the increasingly crowded field. Over the previous five years, Nailite had grown at a compound rate of over 20 percent a year while the industry grew a little over 10 percent. Nailite was not only getting its share of new business, it was increasing its market share. Still, I wasn't surprised when Wasserman asked me to arrange the workshop. He had been a client for a long time, and I had seen him operate. He likes to stay ahead of the game. Whereas unearthing brand-new competitive advantages appeared unlikely, he knew we could certainly quantify and sharpen the ones he already had. He made it clear that cutting prices was not an option. I was thrilled to hear this kind of commitment.

There was another reason I had qualms about Nailite. At the beginning of the workshop, I could sense that some of the Nailite people were mildly skeptical of what we were doing. That, of course, only made me more determined to achieve great results from our workshop session. (And by the end of the session, even the skeptics were telling me how surprised and pleased they were at what they had learned.)

As the workshop session progressed, and Wasserman's earnest participation became apparent to everyone, the skeptics in the crowd paid more attention and became very enthusiastic. Before long, we had a growing list of competitive advantages.

For homeowners—who are, after all, the folks who live with the product—the Nailite team put together an impressive list of reasons to choose Nailite over the competition:

- Eighty percent of customers surveyed chose Nailite siding over natural cedar, brick, or stone.
- Nailite will save you up to $10,000 in maintenance costs over ten years, compared with natural materials.
- Customers can select from 40 percent more products than the nearest competitor.
- Only company with a choice of two different warranties.
- Increases home resale value.
- Custom colors in small quantities.
- Wind-load rating that is five times greater than vinyl siding.
- Polymer is environmentally friendly and biodegradable.
- Half the cost of real cedar.
- Average maintenance of only one hour per year, to hose off dirt and grime.

- Can change color of house by painting without voiding warranty.

But while the research we did after the workshop revealed that homeowners are likely to choose Nailite over competing products, they don't buy the product directly. Like all manufacturers of building supplies, Nailite sells only to distributors who then sell to contractors, who in turn supply the products to architects, builders, and homeowners. Even if the end user prefers the product, distributors and contractors have to first make it available for them. And the reasons distributors and contractors choose Nailite differ substantially from what the end user wants. For them, the product isn't something to live with; it is something to move quickly and profitably. Because distributors are Nailite's first-line customers, Nailite must provide the sales message for contractors and end users.

Research showed that the four attributes deemed most important to distributors in selecting a molded plastic siding company were:

- Dependable service and delivery
- High sales volume
- High profit margin
- Advertising support from the manufacturer

When Nailite researched contractors, it found they had a different set of priorities. The attributes that contractors valued most among makers of molded plastic siding were:

- Product durability
- Cost advantages over real wood, stone, or brick
- Most realistic in appearance

The contractors also cited these attributes as being important:

- Experience in injection molding
- Job referrals from manufacturer
- Company-provided tools to help sell and promote the product

While Nailite scored well with its distributors and contractors, so did its major competitors, Alcoa and CertainTeed. Among distributors, Nailite was rated at or near the top. But among contractors, CertainTeed and Alcoa both outranked Nailite in attributes deemed most important. The category killers had been getting their message across to contractors better than Nailite had.

Nailite continued fine-tuning its competitive advantages for each market segment but decided to put more focus on the contractor group. It wasn't enough for homeowners to rate Nailite's product best, or for distributors to be happy to have it in their pipelines. Contractors are the ones who install the stuff—and that is where Nailite had some work to do.

If you have different levels of customers, you have to identify and tout different competitive advantages tailored for each of them. After our workshop, Nailite's team came out believing it can match or exceed its competitors when providing what contractors want most. Now it has to make sure contractors know that Nailite can do everything the industry giants can do, as well as or better than they can. The Nailite case proves that you don't always have to make significant changes in your product or operations to take on powerful competitors. You merely have to educate yourself about who your customers are—those on the front line, the end users, and everyone in between. What can you give him or her that no one else can? And how do you communicate those advantages?

When Wasserman asked me to conduct the competitive advantage workshop, neither of us knew where it might all lead. After all, Nailite's sales and revenue were increasing at twice the industry average, and customers love the product. But a soft spot was found, one that might not otherwise have been identified until significant damage was done. And we found it long before a price war could emerge.

Sometimes your best competitive advantage is finding out when someone is gaining on you—and doing something about it fast. If you have to resort to price cutting, you may have already lost the battle.

TEAR A PAGE FROM THEIR PLAYBOOK

No matter what your industry, you should always keep your eye on the most successful category killers. After all, the big-box guys occasionally think outside of the box. You can often emulate their smart moves, even if you lack their clout and capital. Take the advertising industry, which is now dominated by a few huge, global companies, such as WPP, Omnicom, and Interpublic. They have the staffs and resources to service the world's largest companies in markets around the globe, providing them with everything from PR to film production. They can also serve small clients through their many subsidiaries.

But their size and diversity don't protect them from one of the biggest problems all agencies face—the best way to bill clients. For decades, agencies charged on the basis of billings. The agency charged a percentage of the amount their clients paid to television stations, newspapers, magazines, and so on, to run their ads. But major advertisers began balking at those fees as soon as they realized they had little to do with sales results. An advertiser might spend a fortune on a bad campaign, yet the ad agency that created it would still make out on the billings. Smaller agencies, whose smaller clients might not bill much in advertising, found it difficult to grow without landing a whale or two to ensure high billings. Not an easy task. The hardest job in any advertising agency is to nail down new business.

Eventually, agencies began to bill like lawyers—for the time and labor involved in creating a campaign and placing the ads. Of course, this system isn't ideal, either. Agencies aren't crazy about it, because the only way they can generate more revenue is to charge clients more for time and labor. Keen competition keeps a lid on the fees agencies can charge.

Advertisers aren't totally happy with the fee arrangement either, because it isn't linked to the quality or the success of the ad campaign. Sure, a lousy campaign could cost an agency a major client, but only after the client has already paid through the nose for the campaign development.

Now different forms of compensation are beginning to emerge. One of the folks suggesting them is an industry bigwig, Andy Berlin, co–chief executive of WPP agency Red Cell. He stunned advertisers and agencies alike at the 2005 management conference of the American Association of Advertising Agencies by suggesting a radical change in the way advertising is priced. It boils down to pay for performance: The better the ads do for the buyer, the more the agency gets paid.

Berlin suggested some baby steps in that direction— first changing TV advertising rates to reflect their popularity with viewers. Since television stations risk losing viewers with every ad, station owners want ads that keep viewers tuned in, rather than reaching for the remote. It makes sense, then, Berlin suggested, for TV stations to refigure their rate schedules so that advertising that retains viewers costs less than advertising that chases them away. Google, the category killer in Internet search engines, already employs this strategy. Marketers pay Google less for ads that Google customers like, and more for ads they don't.

Red Cell's Seattle office already offers clients its version of compensation based on success. As producer of its own late-night television program, called *Rainier Vision,* sponsored by Rainier beer, the agency takes the risk for the cost of the show—but owns the rights to it. If the show flops, the advertiser has been spared the expense of production. If it succeeds, the agency can charge rates based on higher viewership.

So far, only one major advertiser insists on strict pay-for-performance deals from its advertising agencies— Procter & Gamble, which spends more on advertising than any other company in the world (over $2 billion on TV ads alone). If the ads boost product sales by a fat margin, the agencies are paid more. If the ads fail to boost sales, the agencies get less.

THE SKIN GAME

Putting your own skin in the game is risky, of course. You have to have both the ability and the confidence to bet on yourself. And you can't afford to be wrong, at least not often. In Chapter 2, we discussed how you can win customers by pointing out ways you can actually save them money if they pick you over the competition. Matching pay to performance is another way. The more money your client makes because of what you do for him, the more you will get paid.

If you are in a service business and the category killer

is beating you on price, you can also try the pay-for-performance tactic. Lawyers have been thriving for years on contingency fees. They get paid only if they win and then take a hefty percentage of the award. Real estate agents collect from clients only if they sell houses. Some investment companies charge clients a percentage of their portfolio gains. If the portfolio goes down, they suffer, too.

Offering to accept pay for performance, instead of fees, amounts to your personal guarantee of results. It's a solid competitive advantage, especially against the big guys who shy away from such risk. I have offered to sell my consulting services based on performance—charge nothing up front, but agree to a percentage of new revenues generated as a result of my work. As soon as they do the math, the clients opt for the fees instead. But merely making the offer has often been a deal closer for me. The CEO of a southeastern hospital was shopping for some help marketing one of the facility's specialties. He told me he had asked three marketing companies if they would put their money where their mouths were and accept a pay-for-performance arrangement. All the other marketing firms emphatically said no, they simply couldn't do that. I eagerly volunteered.

I got the assignment. Even though he opted to pay my straight fee, it was my willingness to put sweat equity into the project that convinced him to choose my firm.

CREATE A COMPETITIVE ADVANTAGE CULTURE

Competitive advantages don't just happen. They require planning, decision making, and implementation. Your company probably holds retreats to discuss strategic planning, marketing, teamwork, and so forth. I strongly recommend that companies large and small consider company retreats that focus on competitive advantage, and to consider these questions:

- What actions does your company take to create a culture that seeks out competitive advantages?
- Do your statistics back up what you say are your competitive advantages?
- When was the last time you looked closely at the competition? Do you evaluate your own competitive advantages against those of your next two competitors? (In other words, are you outrunning the other guy and still getting away from the bear?)
- What can you do, beginning today, to instill a competitive advantage mind-set in your organization?
- How often have you let price be your differentiator? Are you doing it now as a conscious strategy or as a default position?
- What competitive advantages do you currently enjoy that can disappear very quickly if the competition decides to zero in on you? What would you do to protect your market share?

CHAPTER 5

Competitive Advantages Are Not Simply Strengths

FOR MOST COMPANIES, LARGE OR SMALL, A COMPETItive advantage is rarely unique and not often sustainable over an extended period of time. But smart companies remain on the alert for new competitive advantages to develop and promote. They spend a lot of time on customer research. They pay attention to the competition and develop strong competitive intelligence. They may even take over a competitor with a strong competitive advantage or hire away the people responsible for developing it.

Good companies are also built on solid footings. They have all the strengths they need to compete: quality, knowledgeable people, and good customer service, to name a few. But a strength is not a competitive advantage; remember, you need strengths just to be in business at all. There is nothing unique or even noteworthy about characteristics such as trust, responsiveness, and longevity. Rarely will they ever close a sale.

Strengths are important, of course, but they are not differentiators. Yet in their eagerness to draw attention to themselves, companies will often brag about assets that are commonplace and trite. Consider your company's "rich history and tradition," for example. If your company has been family-owned and -operated for 150 years, who cares? Does the average Bud drinker care that August Busch III is running the company and his son is the heir apparent? Bud's manufacturing, marketing, and distribution are its competitive advantages, not the Busch bloodline.

But vanity is a fact of life in business, big or small. I have seen dozens of companies make much too big a deal of family ownership. Yet it seldom means much—if anything—to the customer. I cringe whenever I see or hear an amateurish television commercial delivered by a business owner. The message to the consumer (if he or she hasn't already switched channels) is this: We're too cheap, too vain, or too stupid to hire professionals to do our ads, and, on top of that, we really don't have a lot to say. Owners of automobile dealerships seem particularly prone to this temptation.

My favorite example, though, is a distributor of home heating oil located in the Northeast (name withheld so as not to further embarrass the owners). The distributor's television ad opens with a group of gray-haired men sitting in a beat-up, old office. Then the camera pans to a driver attending a delivery truck (your teenager could do a better job with a Minicam). The message the company is trying to convey is that it offers emergency service twenty-four hours a day and has been a family business for generations. But almost all heating oil distributors maintain round-the-clock emergency service, and the fact that the company has been around for a while means little to the customer.

I do give the distributor some credit, however, because most companies make *no* effort to communicate their most basic deliverables. They assume that the customers already know them, but our research shows otherwise. As I tell my clients, "If you do something that your competitors do, but you talk about it before they do, then for a while it can be a competitive advantage."

Before you fall for a TV ad salesman's blather about how great you'd look on the tube, ask yourself what it will do for your business. What competitive advantage are you selling? (And being a bigger blowhard than your competitors doesn't count!)

Does the fact that you have been in business decades longer than your competitors ever matter? It depends. If those decades add up to more experience and transactions, then talk about that. But consistent family management alone is no guarantee of anything. The success rate of second- and third-generation family businesses is not great. There are too many examples of "shirtsleeves to shirtsleeves in two generations." Customers might even perceive such nepotism as a competitive *disadvantage*. (As may stockholders, too.)

I understand why owners and CEOs, especially of small businesses, like to brag that they have been around awhile: to reassure clients of their commitment to the business. Fine. But I think there is a limit.

For example, I wouldn't be the first customer of a new general contractor. If he has been in business, say, ten years, and has a long list of references, I will feel a lot more comfortable hiring him. But I am not sure it matters if he has been around twenty, thirty, or more years. The point is simple: Longevity may be a competitive advantage if you're competing against someone with next to no experience, but it won't matter much if your competitors also have a good track record—albeit a shorter one.

ARMS AND THE MAN

I often use a military analogy to illustrate the difference between competitive strengths and competitive advantages. Strengths include up-to-date armament, plenty of ammunition, and a strong standing army. They are the defensive weapons you need just to set foot on the battlefield. Competitive advantages, on the other hand, would include target-seeking missiles, stealth aircraft, and the ability to drop troops behind enemy lines. They are your offensive weapons, needed to conquer new territory (i.e., increase market share). Too many companies think that their troops and ammo are sufficient to storm the marketplace, losing sight of the fact that most competitors have similar troops and ammo.

Competitive advantages can be fleeting. Only monopolies and near-monopoly companies have those that endure. In most other cases, competitive advantages can last months or years, but seldom decades. Unless your competitors are totally asleep, they will cotton on to why you are taking business from them. They will try to imitate, duplicate, or even surpass your current competitive advantage, if they can. If not, they may buy you out.

Suppose your competitive advantage is that you provide customer support all day—every day but Sunday. A competitor might go 24/7, killing your competitive advantage. But it is important to keep in mind that just because a competitive advantage might not last is no reason not to exploit it while the opportunity exists. For a few years, Continental had an ad campaign that boasted "the youngest fleet in the industry." To the frequent flyer, that translates into safer, more comfortable planes and fewer mechanical delays. Of course, other airlines buy new aircraft every day. In fact, I recently heard Continental's song change a bit to "We have one of the youngest fleets" in the industry. While the advantage was fleeting, the carrier was smart to get the word out while it could.

Another example of exploiting a temporary competitive advantage comes from my client Arrow Environmental Services, Inc. Arrow is a pest-control company based in Sarasota that also provides lawn maintenance and renovation service, irrigation services, and interior foliage design systems. As the only pest-control company in a four-county radius to offer all of those services, Arrow enjoys a competitive advantage over the competition.

Yet its competitors may, over time, catch up. They could add lawn services along with pest control. In the meantime, however, my client is expanding its customer base. And that fact alone gives him another competitive advantage—widespread visibility. Some customers feel a lot more comfortable dealing with a company that also services the neighbors.

KEEP ONE EYE FIXED ON THE COMPETITION

Finding and exploiting competitive advantages is not a part-time enterprise. You need to develop a corporate culture that replenishes competitive advantages. And you need to keep a constant eye on the competition. In fact, superior competitive intelligence is in itself a competitive advantage. In my youth, I dated a pro football player who spent hours each week watching film footage of the competition. Coaches and players often look for weaknesses in their opponents and try to devise plays to exploit them. And they're not the only ones. I know several sports-fanatic CEOs who will watch game replays all week, searching for their favorite teams' advantages, but won't spend an hour doing the same kind of research on their business competitors.

Competitive advantage is not just clever advertising. Ads may get you noticed, but they won't do anything for sales unless your customers believe in your product or service. You have to give them reasons to choose you. You have to build confidence. Tired marketing messages won't do that.

Auto manufacturers spend hundreds of millions of dollars a year in advertising, in an effort to move mountains of metal through the showroom doors. Many of the ads are entertaining but have very little to say about the new cars—usually because there isn't really much new or remarkable about them.

"This is not your father's Oldsmobile" was a catchy slogan and campaign for General Motors many years ago, but it failed to sell cars. Where was the competitive advantage? The "new" Olds may have been different from the old Olds, but it was not any better. In fact, it was worse. The Oldsmobile, first made in 1897, had once stood for reliability, but that reputation died a long time ago. Toyota, Honda, and other foreign models were demonstrably more reliable than the tired old Olds, and their resale values proved it.

Today, Oldsmobile has joined the Edsel and the Nash Rambler in Detroit's dustbin. In 2004, when the last Oldsmobile rolled off General Motors' assembly line, few people mourned its passing.

Contrast that with Ford's new Mustang. Rather than

dusting off the old 1960s Mustang, making a few cosmetic changes and relying solely on nostalgia to win customers, Ford engineers set about designing and building a new car that would be as sporty, good-looking, and economical as the original. It would have the spirit of the old Mustang without being a corny remake. The Mustang for 2005 is bigger, stronger, and more driver-friendly than its forebear, yet it is as affordable as the old version. (Models start at about $19,000.)

Ford felt it really had something to crow about, and critics agreed. One wrote, "There hasn't been a new model in years that's hit the sweet spot the same way the '05 Mustang does." Ford cranked up production and advertising accordingly. To catch the flavor of the late '60s, a digitally resurrected Steve McQueen starred in the TV ads. Sales took off. In the first half of 2005 alone, despite limited availability, the new Mustang was Ford's hottest-selling car. Sales totaled 96,011, up 31 percent from a year earlier.

In its category of inexpensive, sporty coupes, the stylish, peppy Mustang has a decided competitive advantage (a Mustang convertible hit showrooms in 2006).

Building a new car from scratch is an expensive and risky way to develop a competitive advantage, but it's not the only way. Ford has cashed in on its F-150 pickup truck not by remodeling it but by touting how tough it already was. The F-150 pickup has been America's best-selling truck for twenty-eight years.

In 2003, Ford gave the new F-150 the biggest marketing launch in its history. The star of the "Built Ford Tough" campaign wasn't a classic screen star but six steel bolts that join the truck frame to ensure that the box and cargo area are firmly secured to the truck. No other manufacturer does the same.

The message was: If Ford uses bolts this strong—strong enough to hold up the entire 5,000-pound truck—then the entire vehicle must be just as strong. Ford sold more than 900,000 F-150 trucks in 2004, another industry record. In the trucking business, toughness counts.

MAKING THE MOST OF YOUR STRENGTHS

At my seminars, I ask CEOs and other executives in attendance to list what they think is the most important competitive advantage of their companies. These are the ten most common responses I hear:

- Good customer service
- Quality
- Reputation
- Good results
- Our employees
- Knowledgeable staff
- Consistent management
- Responsiveness
- Innovativeness
- Trust

All good companies have these qualities or they wouldn't be in business long. They play solid defense. But that doesn't mean you can't demonstrate that your strengths are superior to your competitors'. Do you recall Eliza Doolittle singing "Show Me" in *My Fair Lady*? "Words, words, words, I'm so sick of words!"

Just as Eliza wanted Henry Higgins to *show* her he loves her, your customers need you to show them what you mean by quality, good service, and the rest. And this is where research comes in. Dazzle them with details. Here are some examples of how you can make those ten strengths much more meaningful for customers. In some cases, the statements may be competitive advantages, and in others, simply good competitive positioning:

INSTEAD OF SAYING WE PROVIDE:	CONSIDER SAYING THIS:
Good customer service	"Our electronics sales and service business promises to return all calls within one hour of being received and, if necessary, will have a technician at your location within six hours." *Be specific.*
Quality	"Last year, less that half of 1 percent of our customers returned one of our products." *If your product is as good as you say, you won't have a lot of returns.*

Reputation

"Over 90 percent of our business comes from referrals." *Don't go flashing around pictures of the company founder. Show your potential customers how satisfied your long-term customers are.*

Good results

"After switching to our product line, our customers reported an average 25 percent boost in manufacturing productivity." *Keep accurate measurements of how your customers benefit from using your products or services.*

Our employees

"Our engineers have a minimum of fifteen years of experience, twice that of our nearest competitor." *Simply stating "Our people are the best in the industry" won't cut it. Back up your boast with meaningful numbers. Warning: Never say your employees have a* combined *150 years of experience. Customers picture two old guys sitting at a desk. Use minimum or average terms of experience instead.*

Knowledgeable staff	"Our interior design firm has won more awards than any other design firm in the region." *If your company has won industry awards, or your staff members hold impressive credentials, make sure your customers know about them.*
Consistent team	"You can rely on our sales and service people; our turnover rate is only 2 percent a year. Our customer reps are all veterans, so when you call us, ordering, delivery, and billing will go a lot more smoothly because the person at the other end of the line knows you." *Familiarity breeds contentment. Customers will have more confidence in selecting your company if they deal with the same sales and service people.*
Responsiveness	"We guarantee that your orders will be confirmed and shipped within three hours of placement. Your calls will be returned within twenty minutes; our technicians will be on site the next day."

Responding quickly to customers' needs will win you business. But make sure you can deliver. Making claims you can't meet is worse than not making them at all.

Innovativeness

"We have five patents pending on our new products, twice as many as our competitors. We invite you to come and see our state-of-the-art manufacturing operation." *It's never enough to simply say your company is "innovative." Who would admit otherwise? Dazzle your customers with your achievements.*

Trust

"Our customer-retention rate is 95 percent, twice that of our nearest competitor." *Don't keep stats like these a secret. Every time I ask a CEO group how many of them have a high retention rate, about 75 percent raise their hands. I then ask, "How many of you tout it to your prospects?" Only a few hands go up. They are blowing an easy opportunity to gain the confidence of new prospects.*

DOES ETHICS COUNT FOR ANYTHING?

At almost all my seminars, I'll get a question that goes something like this: "Who is to know if we exaggerate, or fudge some numbers? Our competitors do it all the time."

The question reminds me of an article I read by Christopher Buckley, who reminisced about running a charter boat during his summer breaks from college. (The yacht was owned by his dad, William F.) Buckley recounts that as a special treat for his well-heeled clients, he would sometimes haul up a lobster trap and take a lobster or two for dinner. To cover the cost of the purloined crustaceans, he would put a bottle or two of liquor in the trap before dropping it back in the water—he considered it a fair exchange.

After hauling up a pot one afternoon and helping himself to a couple of lobsters, Buckley asked the wealthy cheapskate who hired the boat to hand over a bottle of Scotch to put in the trap. The man looked around at the empty ocean and asked, "Who is to know?"

Sometimes it can be very tempting to cheat or lie—in business and in life. Especially when it's easy to get away with it. We all know golfers who never seem to have a bad round (at least on their own scorecards). After all, "Who's to know?" But in business at least three parties will usually know when you are lying or cheating—you, your employees, and, eventually, your competitors. (Not to mention the authorities.)

My advice to the sorely tempted is always the same: "Don't claim it if it ain't so." For me, it's less a matter of ethics than of common sense. Instead of "Who's to know?" you should consider the consequences and ask, "What happens if we get caught?"

During one seminar in Seattle, I was discussing this very issue with a workshop group. I was pointing out the folly of making false claims in order to create a competitive advantage. "Your competitors will make sure your customers know when you lie," I said. One CEO nearly leaped from his seat. "You are so right!" he blurted out. "And I can prove it."

He explained that in his business he buys large quantities of packing tape and had always used the same source. "My supplier's chief competitor kept knocking on my door, but I stayed with the guy with whom I had a relationship," he said. "Finally, one day the competitor begged me to spend ten minutes with him in my warehouse. He asked me to take a look at a roll of the tape I was currently using and a roll of his tape. Both rolls were labeled '100 feet.' Then he asked me to measure the tapes by walking them across the floor. The tape I had been using for years measured only eighty-five feet in length, 15 percent less than the other tape. My old supplier had been cheating me for years! The competitor immediately got my account."

Never underestimate the ability of your competitors to catch you in a lie or to find out that you are cheating. They are in the same business as you are, and when they get wise to your tricks they will pass that information along to your customers, their own lawyers—and, in some cases, relevant authorities.

In its days of exponential growth in the 1990s, Microsoft resorted to some shady practices, including strong-arming some customers from using rival products like Netscape, and overcharging some computer makers for its Windows operating system. Companies like Sun Microsystems, IBM, and Gateway, among others, did more than quietly seethe. Wouldn't you? They passed on their complaints to investigators and the result was a massive federal antitrust suit, which Microsoft lost. From 2003 to 2005 alone, the company has doled out well over $4 billion to resolve the case, including almost $2 billion to bitter rival Sun Microsystems.

It's just as you tell your kids about lying and cheating: Once you start, it's hard to stop. I am not going to moralize about ethics here. But a little bit of ethics would have gone a long way in preventing the corporate heads of Enron, WorldCom, Tyco, Adelphia, and others from facing long jail sentences.

Ethical standards come from the top, and in their absence, it's a short walk from being an unethical company to being a criminal one. In the wake of the Enron collapse, for example, a memo was unearthed quoting one manager, "I wish we would get caught. We're such a crooked company." That employee got his wish.

Business ethics was not something Enron or its CEO, Jeff Skilling, ever paid much heed to. When Skilling was a student at the Harvard Business School, a professor asked his class what a CEO should do if he discovered that his company was producing a product that might be harmful, or even fatal, to consumers.

Skilling was quick to respond. "I'd keep making and selling the product," he said to the professor. "My job as a businessman is to be a profit center and maximize return to the stockholders. It's the government's job to step in if a product is dangerous." It didn't matter if customers, employees, even the CEO's own family might get sick or die from using that product.

In other words, it's fine to inflict harm, or even death, as long as the company makes money and gets away with it. It's up to Uncle Sam to put a stop to the carnage. A nationwide survey of MBA students some years later indicated that Skilling was hardly alone in his thinking. In 2001, some 2,000 new MBAs from thirteen top business schools were asked what a company's top priorities should be. Three of four said that the most important goal was to "maximize value for shareholders." Only one-third of the newly minted MBAs, tomorrow's corporate leaders, put a high priority on producing high-quality goods and services.

The mantra "maximizing shareholder value" has often been used as a fig leaf to conceal some top managers' real motives—to get filthy rich, to hell with the customer.

Thankfully, they are a small minority, and thankfully, they usually get caught.

IS GOOD ETHICS
A COMPETITIVE ADVANTAGE?

Clarence P. Cazalot, CEO of Marathon Oil Corp., has long taken the high road when it comes to corporate ethics. He believes it pays off. In a speech before the Conference Board's 2002 ethics conference, he said: "Our companies are dedicated to being sustainable companies. That is, companies that build long-term shareholder value while being a responsible corporate citizen. And we believe the only way to achieve that is to incorporate economic, environmental, and social codes of conduct into our business strategy. We are determined to conduct our business day in and day out, from top to bottom, and at home and abroad, with honesty, integrity, and decency to our customers, our suppliers, our shareholders, and one another. . . . In other words, we don't lie, we don't cheat, and we don't steal. . . . Integrity is a competitive advantage."

Cazalot went on to describe several instances where Marathon slipped up. The company made false claims about some products. And some mistakes were made in refining so that some of its propane contained impurities. Marathon acted quickly to right the wrongs, notify customers, and alert employees of the lapses. "When you're going to have to eat crow, it's best to eat it while it's still young and tender," Cazalot said.

He also pointed out that Marathon adheres to conservative financial strategies and transparent financial reporting. The payoff? Marathon was able to raise more than $1 billion for acquisitions at below-market rates from a syndicate of underwriters that did put a premium on the company's integrity.

Exemplary ethics can pay dividends. But it's not really a competitive advantage. You are not likely to win many new customers because you are known as the Goody Two-Shoes in your industry. And, because people are only human, even the most ethical of companies slip up occasionally or have skeletons in the closet. It is tempting fate to hold yourself out as holier than thou.

In the wake of the Enron and WorldCom fiascoes, for example, the giant accounting firm PwC (PricewaterhouseCoopers) decided to make hay out of the misfortunes of rival Arthur Andersen, which had been the auditor of Enron and WorldCom. PwC ran a television ad touting its own integrity. The camera closes in on a group of golfers, who are bawling out a fellow duffer for trying to cheat on his golf score. The message was the importance of trust.

Soon after, however, some skeletons in PwC's own closet began rattling. PwC had been the auditor for Tyco International, while Dennis Kozlowski was diving into the company cookie jar up to his ankles. PwC was also the auditor for AIG, the target of another major probe into corporate fraud. PwC was even fined $41 million by the federal government for overcharging travel expenses. Where's that trust, guys?

It's worth noting, however, that companies that enjoy

strong competitive advantages are often among the most ethical in their industries. They can afford to be. They don't have to cut corners. And they realize that a company that rewards the good guys and punishes the bad ones in its ranks will have happier, more productive employees.

"Ethical behavior is directly proportional to competitive advantage," writes Mark Goulston, M.D., senior VP of Emotional Intelligence at Sherwood Partners. In *The CEO Refresher*, Goulston makes his point with Bill Gates. In the 1990s, Microsoft was hardly a paragon of ethics. "Bill Gates, Entrepreneur, may have been tempted to 'stack the deck' in his favor to guarantee winning," writes Goulston. "Now with giant successes in the can, respect and esteem from non-ethically challenged pals like Warren Buffett, and innocent trust from his young children causing him to 'want to be a better man,' Bill Gates, The Sequel, is aspiring to become the ethical elder statesman of technology."

Goulston sums it all up nicely: "The greater the competitive advantage, the easier it is to be honest." Enough said. Work on your competitive advantages and all kinds of good things will happen.

REPLACE YOUR CLICHÉS WITH
COMPETITIVE ADVANTAGES

Your customers need to know what makes your company special, from the products/services you offer to the ways in which you deal with your customers. What messages are they getting now? Review your marketing and sales materials, including a printout of your Web site home page. Now underline the clichés and tired, subjective language—such as "We deliver quality and great customer service." See what you have left. Is the prospective customer getting any message at all about your competitive advantages?

For the words you underlined, are there measurements that could turn those tired phrases into valid selling points? For example, instead of "We have knowledgeable and experienced employees," what might you say that describes the level of experience and knowledge of your staff? How many years have they averaged on the job? What awards have they won?

Make a list of the products/services that you provide and their competitive advantages—including the strengths your competitors may not have. See if you can come up with metrics that make your advantages and strengths pop out versus the competition. Say your product is chemical free. Or you offer your customers payment options that your competitors don't match. Or you offer the best warranty in the business, or respond quicker than the competition when troubles arise. Can you quantify those advantages for your customer? Do they know that they can save 3 percent on annual interest by choosing you? Do they know your product is 100 percent organic? Do they know your warranty is good for twenty-five years, or that your average response time is just three hours?

Which advantages and strengths do you already measure that can support claims that your competitors cannot make? If you are a supplier, for example, you already know how long it takes for an order to be fulfilled and delivered. How does that performance stack up against the competition? Is it worth bragging about, or improving, so it becomes a competitive advantage?

Which advantages and strengths do you need to start measuring in order to prove your claims if you need to?

The key is to focus not simply on your product/service itself but on all aspects of your relationship with your customer. Every one of your deliverables offers an opportunity for a competitive advantage or competitive positioning.

CHAPTER 6

Competitive Positioning
Seize the High Ground First

SOMETIMES A COMPETITIVE ADVANTAGE IS NOT really a competitive advantage at all—but can pass for one. Let's say that 95 percent of your business comes from referrals. Maybe some competitors can say the same thing, too, but don't. So you make the claim first, and make it loudly. By the time the competitors make that same claim, if they do at all, they will be playing catch-up.

I call this tactic, which I've touched upon briefly in earlier chapters, "competitive positioning." You really don't have a competitive advantage, but your customer thinks you do because you are making a valid claim that your competitors have yet to beat.

The interior designer introduced earlier in the book

stresses to his clients that he uses computer-aided design, which will save them up to ten days of construction time. Most designers now use the same technology, but most assume that their customers know what it enables. My client doesn't make such assumptions. He explains how it saves his customers time, and how the technology allows for last-minute changes to be made. By competitively positioning a "strength," he's better able to close deals. Never assume your customers know how the technology or processes you offer helps them in the transaction. More often than not, they don't know as much as they should.

Consider the marketing of Off!, the popular insect repellent that is especially effective against mosquitoes. Made by SC Johnson Wax, Off! is by no means a unique product. Its active ingredient is DEET, a chemical repellent patented by the U.S Army in 1946. At least a half-dozen other companies use DEET or another chemical agent, picaridin, in their repellents. They are all effective in getting all kinds of mosquitoes to buzz off (though repellents that use natural substances are less effective).

How do you make your product stand out when it is virtually the same as your competitors'? The makers of Off!, aware that the deadly West Nile virus is transmitted by mosquitoes, prominently advertise that the product "repels mosquitoes that may carry WEST NILE VIRUS." Of course, so do HourGuard, DEET Plus, Cutter, Repel, and other insect repellents. But Off! states its claim boldly on the label, playing on one of the most basic of human emotions, fear. Off! is positioned as the defender against

West Nile disease. As a parent shopping for insect sprays, which one would catch your eye on the market shelf?

Coors Brewing started a major campaign in the fall of 2004 promoting its light beer as the "coldest-tasting beer in the world." Wait a minute. Beer is beer, and ice is ice. Beer can only get so cold before it freezes. What makes Coors taste colder? Coors wanted to remind consumers that its beer is cool-brewed and not pasteurized. Anheuser-Busch, Miller, and other major beer companies do not cool-brew their beer, so Coors claims it as a competitive advantage. Does it make the beer taste better? Who knows? But it sounds good, especially on a hot summer day. Coors positioned its beer as the coldest-tasting on the market, and sales spiked.

Companies in the airline industry are eager to position themselves as more than a commodity. Competitive positioning is often the best way to beat this status. A few years ago, when Continental Airlines was competing against several other carriers for the lucrative South and Latin American markets, someone realized they offered more than 500 flights from the United States to South and Latin America per week. By advertising 500 weekly flights, Continental conditioned the traveling public to think of it first when flying to South and Latin America. Continental positioned itself as the principal carrier to those destinations, and won a lot of traffic as a result. Note that Continental didn't claim to have "the most flights to Latin America," only that they had 500 per week.

If you have the "most" options for your customers, say

so. And if you don't, state the quantity if it is impressive enough. As long as your competitors give you the opening, seize that competitive position.

Many years ago when I was product manager for the Caribbean for Eastern Airlines, I was helping to launch the San Juan hub just as American Airlines was doing the same thing. American jumped out ahead of us and declared on billboards and radio that they had "more flights to the Caribbean" than any other carrier.

At first we were worried that American might steal our thunder. But I took a closer look at the numbers, comparing American's schedule with our own at Eastern, and found this juicy bit of data: American had more flights, but we at Eastern had more wide-bodied aircraft in that market. I did the math and found that we actually had "more seats to the Caribbean" than American did. Advantage: Eastern. We wasted little time using that fact to better position ourselves in the market.

Moral: Economists and politicians aren't the only folks who can use numbers to say what they want. You can, too.

BEWARE THE SHADOW EFFECT

Airlines spend a lot of money and effort on passenger surveys, trying to find out what will put more people on their planes. When I started my airline career at Pan Am, fares were the same on virtually all carriers, so price was not an issue. We focused on food, service, comfort, and so on. After countless surveys, we began to see an intriguing pattern. If the flights left and arrived on time, passengers felt generally positive about things like food, service, and comfort. If the flights were delayed, however, passengers gave us low marks for everything, from check-in to after-dinner coffee.

The "shadow effect" of on-time arrivals and departures was an eye-opener. It told us that being on time was so important to passengers that little else mattered. If the flights were on time, we had happy passengers. If they were late, they rated everything poorly.

Southwest Airlines has built its extraordinarily successful operation on prompt arrivals and departures. Founders Rollin King and Herb Kelleher started the airline in 1972 with one simple notion: "If you get your passengers to their destinations when they want to get there, on time, at the lowest possible fares, and make darn sure they have a good time doing it, people will fly your airline." It worked.

Southwest's on-time record has long been the envy of the industry, and it consistently ranks in the top three or four. Its boarding system is a model of speed and efficiency—seats are not preassigned, so passengers board like nuns filing into church pews. Southwest also ranks at or near the top in baggage handling, another major concern of passengers. It should be no surprise that for thirty-two straight years, the carrier has operated in the black. No other airline can match that record.

If you focus on the things that your customers care about most, they will keep coming back. Southwest has positioned itself as the budget carrier with the fewest delays. And while some other carriers now match or even beat its low fares, Southwest retains its customers and continues to grow. Passengers expect Southwest to get them to their destinations when it says it will. (In passenger surveys, Southwest also gets high marks for its upbeat flight crews. Perhaps the crews are so cheerful because they get home on time, just as the passengers do.)

Southwest has its imitators, of course. JetBlue, another budget carrier that has managed to stay profitable in the troubled airline industry, does a lot of things that Southwest does, but it does not position itself the same way. Its low fares and on-time records are comparable to those of Southwest, but JetBlue stresses customer service above all else. It also touts its new fleet of Airbus A320 aircraft, outfitted with leather seats, each of which is equipped with a screen offering twenty-four-channel satellite television. All seats are assigned, all travel is ticketless, all fares are one-way, and a Saturday-night stay is never required. It's a budget carrier, but a warm and cuddly one.

I asked David Neeleman, CEO of JetBlue, about his airline's competitive advantages. Neeleman had come to JetBlue from Southwest and knew well its key to success. He tried to go one better. "Our goal is to delight the customer," he said. "Not overpromise in advertising, but let them have the experience. We want our business to come from word of mouth, and a large percentage of it does. Once customers experience JetBlue, they tell friends and family. That's our goal. Obviously, our new planes, extra legroom, et cetera, are all additional competitive advantages. But we focus on real, true customer service, making sure our people make passengers feel special."

I mentioned to Neeleman that competitive advantages like more legroom and free satellite TV are fleeting. At the time of my interview, Delta Song was offering free satellite TV and ample legroom on its flights.

"Yes, but Hewlett-Packard wants to be Dell, but can't," he said. "While Delta has copied us, they can't beat us. They have other challenges and baggage that comes with their history. We are constantly looking at new plans and new ways to delight the customer. We stay connected. We are looking at all kinds of new services. Brand extensions, hotels, rental cars, and so on. We are constantly surveying our customer. We may start surveying every customer, with a reward for filling out the entire form. I am an idea guy. I am constantly flying our airline and others and looking at competition and seeking new ways to do things better. If we see something new, we don't try to catch up, we try to do it better."

"You are always on the lookout for competitive advantages," I said.

"Each week, key managers and I have a three-hour conference call to discuss what are we doing, what they are doing, and how can we do it better," he said.

"Do you think it is possible for a company to prosper without a competitive advantage?" I asked.

"It can survive for a while, but not prosper," he answered. And Neeleman was right. Delta is phasing out Song this year.

If you are running a large company, you already have a lot of support and a large budget to differentiate yourself. Your own marketing people, as well as advertising agencies that are seeking your business, will provide a steady stream of fresh ideas on how to better position and sell your product or service. Of course, your competitors have the same marketing and advertising resources, too. That's why advertising is a multibillion-dollar industry. Large companies can afford to duke it out on TV, radio, in print, and on the Internet to establish brand identity. Still, it's up to you to convince customers to use your bug spray, buy your beer, or fly your airline.

That's tough enough for big companies. But what if you are a small or midsize business and your pockets aren't quite as deep? What if the service you provide is hard to differentiate from that of hundreds of competitors? How do you position yourself to stand out? One way is to come up with impressive numbers.

HELP FOR THE SUPERSIZED

When John C. Johnson, CEO of Holy Cross Hospital in Fort Lauderdale, Florida, asked me to conduct a workshop to help his hospital market its bariatric (gastric bypass) surgery facility, I knew it wasn't going to be easy.

I had no idea how the hospital could differentiate itself from the many other bariatric facilities popping up like mushrooms around the country. What could Holy Cross say about their business that the others couldn't?

I am going into some detail about what happened at Holy Cross because it could serve as a template for many other small and medium-size institutions, regardless of product or service. What helped Holy Cross stand out from the pack was a formidable combination of competitive advantages and competitive positioning statements.

Before the workshop, I did a little homework on bariatric surgery. I found that there are a lot of misconceptions about this form of surgery, and potential patients have to be educated about what it entails. But their numbers are growing. In 2005, about 75,000 people had gastric bypass surgery, up from about 45,000 in 2001. It is not some quickie way to shed unwanted pounds. It involves surgery on the stomach and/or intestines, to limit the amounts of food patients ingest each day. Laymen call it stomach stapling, but it's hardly that crude these days. In fact, in many cases, the procedures are performed using a TV monitor and a laparoscope—a slender tube that is inserted through a small incision in the stomach. There is no need for a large, open incision.

The procedure is recommended only for people aged 15 to 60 who are at least 100 pounds above their ideal weight or who have a body mass index (BMI) above 40. (Someone who is 5 feet, 6 inches tall, for example, would have to weigh about 248 pounds to have a BMI of 40. A six-footer would have to weigh close to 300 pounds.)

Surgery may also be an option for people with a BMI between 35 and 40 who have other health problems, like heart disease, diabetes, hypertension, arthritis, or sleep apnea. I also learned that while bariatric surgery saves and prolongs lives, it is not always covered by insurance. The procedure is tax-deductible, however.

The participants in the workshop included doctors, administrators, and the hospital CEO. Early into the workshop session, I realized that Holy Cross had a lot of sharp scalpels in its drawer. They had already pinpointed their problems and knew what their goals were. When you start out with that kind of focus, good things can happen.

Here were the chief problems that they identified:

- They didn't know how to differentiate themselves from competitors.
- They never developed power selling points in their sales and marketing.
- They had not defined their message.
- They hadn't educated the community about the bariatric program at Holy Cross.

Among their chief goals were these:

- To bring more patients in—specifically, to double the number of patients from 1,000 to 2,000 a year.

- To create a memorable message to be used in sales literature, advertising, and on the Web site.
- To be able to explain bariatric surgery to the target audience in a coordinated, data-driven manner.
- To develop a marketing plan to attract patients for additional subsequent care.
- To create a message so targeted it will save marketing dollars.

During the drill-down session of the workshop, the participants came up with a long list of their competitive advantages. One of them was that the director of U.S. Bariatric (USB), Dr. Robert T. Marema, was a poster child for bariatric surgery. Not only had he undergone the surgery himself and since then maintained a healthy weight, so had two of his own family members. Marema had performed more than twice as many bariatric surgeries as any other surgeon in the state of Florida, had written a textbook on the subject, and had trained more than 300 other bariatric surgeons.

"Tell me more," I said, trying to unearth some more unique characteristics about the director.

"He's cute!" said one woman in the group. I conceded that his being cute might actually be a competitive advantage, especially as Dr. Marema had maintained a healthy weight since his own surgery. But as much of a star as Dr. Marema is, USB had a lot more to brag about. Among the other competitive advantages and positioning statements we uncovered:

- Largest bariatric program in Florida, with more than 4,000 patients served.
- Highest success rate getting insurers to pay for the operation.
- More than twenty-five members of the staff have undergone bariatric surgery at U.S. Bariatric (they have a first-hand understanding of patient concerns).
- Patients are visited frequently by members of the staff.
- Largest staff in the United States dedicated exclusively to bariatric surgery.
- Alternate weight-loss programs offered, including nonsurgical methods.
- Ninety-five percent of patients achieved a healthy body weight.
- Less than 1 percent required a second surgery.
- All of USB's patients receive a lifetime fitness club membership.

All of the above are very important and impressive advantages, but Holy Cross was still looking for that one key positioning statement: a short, clear, memorable phrase, backed up by numbers, that would make it stand out.

Inevitably, we began chatting about fast food and its contribution to the expanding trade of bariatric surgery. "If McDonald's weren't so successful, maybe we wouldn't be here," someone said.

"They don't even display the number of hamburgers sold anymore," someone pointed out. "After they reached

100 billion, the electronic tote signs under the golden arches had no more room!"

"At an average of a quarter pound each, that's 25 billion pounds of burgers already consumed," someone else added. "That gives us a lot of fat to take off."

One surgeon in the group did some quick number-crunching. "We're making a dent, anyway," he said. "At an average of 100 pounds lost per patient and over 4,000 surgeries performed, we've already helped patients lop off about 400,000 pounds of fat."

There it was—the simple, powerful message we had been looking for. USB's patients had lopped off more than 400,000 pounds and were still counting! If you were a potential patient who was 100 pounds overweight, wouldn't that message hit home?

Soon, USB was using those stats in its advertising and Tuesday evening information sessions, and updating them frequently. The ad-response rate rose 120 percent, and the Tuesday night sessions netted more attendees who subsequently became patients.

As of mid-2005, its message read: "Our surgeons have performed weight-loss surgery on more than 5,000 people, helping them to lose more than 660,000 pounds." Do I hear a million?

The program was so successful that Holy Cross CEO Johnson ran similar ads for the hospital's angioplasty and heart surgery operations. Again, the numbers did the talking. Its ads for heart surgery, for example, stressed these competitive advantages:

- Number one in Broward and Palm Beach Counties
- Number one four years in a row
- Number one for heart attack survival
- Number one for angioplasty success

In my presentations, I like to use Holy Cross Hospital and U.S. Bariatric as an illustration of how to use competitive positioning. At one session, a CEO in the audience attested to the effectiveness of Holy Cross's campaign.

"I was so impressed with that ad that I told my wife if I ever have a heart attack don't call 911. Just throw me in the back of the car and get me to Holy Cross."

"Yeah, my wife would do that for me, too," someone joked. "Only she'd drive real slow."

SO BRAG A LITTLE

The nation faces no imminent shortage of investment advisors. Our mailboxes bulge with pitches from banks, brokers, insurance salesmen and estate planners, and accountants to help us with our investments and financial planning.

While a few bad apples have hurt the reputation of this industry, there are also plenty of honest, talented financial advisors, and they have a tougher sell than most folks do in business. They have to separate themselves from the greedy stockbrokers and other so-called advisors who are interested only in selling stocks, bonds, mutual funds, annuities, and other financial products that line their own pockets.

I once took on as a client a financial advisor who was one of the good guys. He was a CPA who got licensed to manage portfolios. His business was doing quite well, but he needed to reach beyond the accounting clients he already had.

"How can I stand out from the pack of other advisors?" he asked.

"Be honest," I said, only half joking. "That will get people's attention."

After we discussed his business for a while, I realized that I was lucky. The client was, of course, honest. But he was also very good at what he did. I had to do some tooth pulling, as the client was a modest man but certainly had the goods to position himself above the pack. His performance as a money manager was exceptional. And he retained almost all his customers. Plus, he had a solid relationship with Fidelity Investments, one of the biggest and most respected financial institutions in the country.

Here are the competitive positioning statements we stressed in his literature and ads:

- Ranked in top ten money managers who outperformed S & P Index three years running
- Retained 98 percent of clients
- Was elected to Fidelity Investments' national board of investment advisors

- Was one of the first to build an alliance with other CPAs to expand practice
- Fastest-growing money manager in the state last three years

Within eighteen months, my client and the CPAs who were part of his alliance doubled his firm's assets under management. He had indeed positioned himself as an honest and talented financial advisor, mainly by doing some justifiable bragging.

DOCTORS YOU CAN VISIT ON DEMAND

The health care industry is obviously thriving, but your family doctor may not necessarily be reaping the rewards. Increased patient loads, soaring malpractice insurance costs, shrinking reimbursements from insurers, and paperwork nightmares are chasing primary care providers into other specialties or out of medicine completely. According to a recent survey in the *Journal of Family Practice*, more than a quarter of primary-care physicians are expected to quit within the next two years. As it is, the average primary-care physician sees a patient every ten minutes, yet his annual income is dropping. The simplest solution—seeing even more patients—invites trouble. The average family doctor already serves 2,500 to 4,000 patients—and more patients means less attention to each and more mistakes.

I raise this issue to illustrate how even anonymous and

overworked family doctors can competitively position themselves. They can actually limit their number of patients but increase the cost that each of them pays. For the patient, the advantage is clear: better, more personalized care. For the doctor, it means more annual income and a lighter patient load.

A recent annual exam with a new doctor alerted me to all this. Last year, I had a bone-density test, but my old doctor never discussed the results with me, despite my frequent requests to learn them. My new doctor, on the other hand, tracked down the test results and informed me they were not good. The readings showed that I was at moderate to severe risk of bone fracture. My original doctor had simply initialed and filed the test results, then forgot about them. Had the doctor alerted me to that fact, I would have sought appropriate treatment (and possibly even canceled my ski trip that year).

My new doctor suggested another test. It was a full eighteen months after the first test, and we were fearful of finding further deterioration, since the condition had never been treated. Fortunately, my scores turned out to be much better than originally reported—it turns out that someone at the bone-density center had made a transcription error. Both the lab and my original doctor had slipped up. Considering his workload, it was hardly surprising. Yet my new doctor had the time and persistence to track down the original report, to talk to the doctor at the bone center, and to find the error. Now I can return to my ski vacations without worrying about my bones. How did my new doctor find the time to straighten things out? Did I just get unusually lucky in selecting him? Hardly.

My new doctor, G. David Onstad, belongs to a physicians' network called MDVIP. Instead of a typical patient load of 3,000 or so patients, MDVIP docs have a maximum of 600. That means I don't have to wait a long time in the doctor's office prior to appointments, and I never feel rushed during visits. I am getting better attention and care, and Dr. Onstad is making more money than he was when he had almost five times the number of patients.

How is this possible? How does he enjoy such a clear competitive advantage over most other family doctors? The simple answer is that he is not competing on price. Patients of doctors enrolled in MDVIP pay $1,500 a year for their services. Insurance or Medicare typically covers additional medical bills other than the annual wellness exam. This surcharge allows the doctor to greatly reduce his patient load. Here's what I get for my $1,500:

- Annual comprehensive physical exam
- Wellness and prevention planning, such as counseling for patients who want to lose weight or quit smoking
- Same- or next-day appointments
- Unhurried visits
- No-waiting, on-time appointments
- Physician availability 24/7
- Enhanced coordination of necessary referrals
- Travel medical services, including access to other MDVIP physicians when you are on the road

- E-mail, fax, and personal pager access
- Prescription facilitation
- Private reception area with amenities
- Nationwide network of physicians available

After their annual physicals, patients are supplied with CD-ROM records of their medical histories, pertinent lab and test results, medications, allergies, and so on. This CD-ROM can easily fit in your wallet. For me, and a lot of other folks, it's $1,500 well spent. I feel reassured that I am getting better, more personal care, and I save more than enough time to compensate for the expense. For my doctor, it's a career-saver. He gets $1,000 from each of his patients ($500 goes to MDVIP), assuring him $300,000 to $600,000 in upfront income, plus insurance reimbursements. Yet he typically sees about fifty patients a week instead of the 150 or more he had previously, when his income was lower.

It should come as no surprise that MDVIP has been swamped with physician applicants, so it can be choosy. Only about one in twenty are accepted into the program. Dr. Edward Goldman, president of the network, told *Fortune Small Business:* "Joining MDVIP does not mean more time on the golf course. Taking good care of a small number of patients is still hard work. Not a lot of doctors are cut out for this kind of practice. Some doctors love the personal interaction with a patient, and others prefer them out cold on an operating table."

Many critics have groused about this luxury medical

care. A handful of congressmen urged that it be banned as a violation of the rules of Medicare. The American Medical Association also raised objections. But eventually, MDVIP won them over. No one else is doing anything to help family doctors survive, or to make it possible for working people to get the care they need without having to spend countless hours in waiting rooms.

The average primary-care doctor makes $153,200 a year, has up to 4,000 patients, spends an average of 10.6 minutes on each visit, and sees 112 patients a week. No wonder their ranks are shrinking so rapidly.

The MDVIP doctor, on the other hand, has an average annual income of $400,000, spends an average of thirty minutes on each visit, and sees fifty patients per week. Elitist? Perhaps. Not everyone can afford the extra fees. But MDVIP makes it financially possible for more doctors to remain in family practice, and for other doctors in the future to choose it as a specialty.

If you were a family doctor, overwhelmed and under-compensated, wouldn't MDVIP appeal to you? Wouldn't you like to position yourself as the doctor who waits for patients?

REACH OUT AND TOUCH SOMEONE

Like the swamped family physician, many owners and operators of small and medium-size businesses have felt helpless as their profits shrank despite their working harder than ever. As the MDVIP example illustrates, the solution does not lie in spending more and more time *in* the business, but *on* the business. For the family doctor, MDVIP is one way to differentiate himself. For the businessman, it helps to reach out to industry and professional associations or consultants who can offer solutions.

One such organization is The Executive Committee (TEC), an international organization of CEOs of middle-market companies. Founded in 1957, its goal is to help its members solve problems, educate themselves, and enhance their lives and businesses.

Among its strong competitive positioning statements:

- It boasts membership of more than 10,000 members, providing one of the world's largest CEO networking opportunities through its member-only Web site.
- TEC-member companies typically experience an annual growth rate that exceeds that of the S & P 500, Fortune 500, and Dow Jones Industrials combined.
- TEC-member companies achieve moderate to high growth at a rate five times that of other small- to medium-sized businesses.
- TEC companies grow approximately 2.5 times faster after their CEOs join TEC than they did before.
- TEC-member companies generate more than $255 billion in annual revenue and represent more than 1.8 million employees in fourteen countries and six continents. These companies include manufacturing, service, wholesale, trade, financial services, and con-

struction firms, providing an unparalleled sampling of business trends.

- Over 99 percent of TEC companies are privately held.

TEC is an organization I not only endorse, but for which I have served as a chair and a speaker. Seventeen years ago, I was the first woman ever hired by TEC to chair a group of CEOs. I am still at it, learning and coaching and conducting seminars.

COME UP WITH SOME GOOD NUMBERS

As I've shown in this chapter, you don't always need to position yourself as the best to beat out your competitors—but you do need some good numbers. You can stack the facts in your favor. McDonald's built its success counting hamburgers sold.

List any measurements you have for your company's deliverables, such as delivery itself. Do you measure the accuracy of shipments, or how quickly you get the orders out the door? Do you measure returns?

You want to make this kind of definitive claim: We have a 98% customer-retention rate.

Or: 90 percent of all oil and gas companies use our machinery.

Or: We install over one million yards of electrical cable each month.

Now, ask yourself, What are you *not* measuring today in your company that could give you competitive positioning statements? Which one of your deliverables, if done right, casts a favorable shadow effect on everything else you do?

Can you tell the difference between true competitive advantages and competitive positioning statements? How many of each can your company come up with? How long will it take for your competitors to mimic your list? What are you doing to ensure that you will have a new list each year?

CHAPTER 7

Dangerous Disparity
The Gap Between What You Assume About Your Customers and What They Really Think

THE RESEARCH I'VE CONDUCTED FOR MY CLIENTS has shown time and again that when they assumed too much about their customers, they usually missed the sales target.

The *only* perceptions that matter are those of your customers. Yet companies often design their marketing, advertising, and sales messages from a purely managerial perspective. They fail to do their homework about what really matters to their customers, and they fail to verify their findings with them. Even if you and your management team can identify what appear to be clear competitive advantages, if you fail to verify them with your customers—or worse, fail to deliver on them—you could be making a major blunder. I call it "dangerous disparity."

There are many ways to cause this disconnect with your customers:

- You use imprecise, vague language that customers don't notice, believe, or understand.
- You claim a competitive advantage that you do not consistently deliver.
- You stress advantages that are not all that important to your customers.
- You fail to stress specific advantages for each of your target markets individually.

Yes, your customers' perceptions could be wrong. But it's up to you to correct them. One of my clients thought he provided good customer service, quality, and delivery. But when we did the research and asked customers to identify his company's *disadvantages,* they rattled off customer service, quality, and delivery as one, two, and three. The frustrating thing was that my client's service, quality, and delivery were measurably better than those of his competitors. But customers thought otherwise, perhaps because these words have been so overused that they have lost any real meaning. Competitive advantages have to mean something positive to customers. They must play an important role in their buying decisions. They must be quantifiable and tied to the customer's bottom line. Above all, they have to be true.

Bragging about the wrong deliverable is another kind of dangerous disparity. Say you tout your good customer service while the customer cares a lot more about delivery time and packing errors. It's like focusing on the outer rings of the target rather than the bull's-eye, where the sales are made. Again, only customer research can save you from going off in the wrong direction.

The most lethal form of dangerous disparity is to claim a competitive advantage and then fail to deliver it. A unit of Waste Management, Inc., in New York bragged that it would contact customers if their refuse was not in the usual place at the usual time for pickup. But, in fact, customers were seldom alerted. Trucks simply rumbled on by. The message amounted to a broken promise to customers, which is bad enough. But the broken promise soon turned into a public relations nightmare.

In one of the areas it serves, the company had to reshuffle weekly pickup dates for many of its customers because of new recycling procedures. But it failed to do an adequate job of informing customers that their refuse would no longer be picked up on the usual day. As a result, many customers called up the company to complain about missed pickups. They were put on hold—for up to an hour. And while waiting, they were treated to a recorded message that repeatedly touted Waste Management's dedication to making every pickup. Callers seethed every time it was repeated.

This kind of dangerous disparity can drive your customers right into your competitors' arms. At the very least, it plants seeds of distrust and dissatisfaction. Customers will begin to drift away without your knowing why. If you claim a competitive advantage, make sure you provide it every time.

MICROSOFT'S BROKEN PROMISES

For years, customers of Microsoft have been screaming about the security holes in Windows, which allow viruses to creep into their operating systems. In 2003, Microsoft said it would make computer security a top priority. CEO Steve Ballmer drew cheers at a conference of some 5,000 important Microsoft customers when he assured them that help was on the way. Security would become a "competitive advantage" for Microsoft, he said. Just be patient.

But at the very same Worldwide Partner Conference a year later, Microsoft had to admit that it had yet to deliver on most of the security patches and updates that Ballmer had promised. The company had done very little to ease its customers' security headaches, and it had done a lot to make them mad and distrustful. Angry customers are hardly ambassadors of your company's products and services. And when they feel entrapped, they can quickly become ex-customers.

Despite its industry dominance, not even Microsoft can afford to mislead its customers while trying to sell them even more wares. Instead of security being a competitive advantage for Microsoft, it has become an albatross. Microsoft knows what its customers want—better security. But there is a perception that Microsoft will not provide it unless it can find a way to profit from it.

I can't say it enough: Be careful of what you assume about your customers. They can often surprise you. EMA, a client of mine I first introduced in Chapter 4, operates hospital emergency rooms—supplying everything from doctors to administration to software. After executives from EMA attended one of my workshops, they put together an inspired list of more than twenty competitive advantages that they believed EMA enjoyed over the competition. These advantages ranged from patient satisfaction to the number of board-certified physicians to the experience of their staff. And at the very top of their list of competitive advantages was the fact that all of the physicians who worked there were equity owners of the company. The EMA team reckoned that physician ownership would be very reassuring to the hospitals that hired them, since the company's principals would be right there on the scene.

After our workshop, we had to verify for EMA which attributes on its list of deliverables were most important to its customers. We set up telephone interviews to ask current and potential customers what they looked for when they were outsourcing their emergency rooms to companies like EMA. This was "blind" research, because the customers (basically, hospital CEOs and others in hospital management) did not know who had commissioned the interviews. We included the names of several of EMA's competitors in the survey, both to disguise the source of the interview and to see how EMA stacked up against the competition.

EMA soon learned something surprising. Its customers placed little value on the fact that EMA is owned by physicians. In fact, that attribute scored dead last.

The customers placed a lot more value on other things that EMA wanted to brag about: patient satisfaction, board-certified physicians, and clinical experience. If EMA had failed to do its research, polling its customers and prospects, it would have gone on playing a tune no one wanted to hear, drowning out its own message. Instead, EMA now stresses those competitive advantages that the customers themselves voted most important. The strategy has paid off. EMA's marketing director told me that once the company got the message right, within six months it won a new hospital contract that added $5 million per year to the company's revenues.

EMA's experience with its customers isn't unusual. Whenever I bring back customer-research findings to clients, I ask them to guess which three attributes were rated highest. Then I ask them to take a stab at which three came in last. To date, no company I've worked with has ever scored six out of six. Again, if you really want to know what your customers think, you have to ask them.

EVEN NONPROFIT STATUS
MAY NOT MATTER

All institutions have to compete to stay alive. Just ask the Visiting Nurse Association of Florida, a nonprofit organization. VNA supplies health care services to the homebound, including skilled nursing care and therapy, patient education, and community and social services for those in need. The organization, while successful for many years, knew it was not attracting as many clients as it should. Visibility wasn't a problem. VNA had been around longer than any other home health care agency in the state, and its public relations efforts were very effective in increasing brand recognition. VNA is the sponsor of a local air show, sponsors a radio program, and hosts a big golf tournament each year. Its message was loud and clear: VNA is alive and well, willing and able to serve in the community. But its message did nothing to address the question "Why us?" Doctors, discharge planners at hospitals, managers of long-term-care facilities, as well as patients and their family members were not turning to VNA for help as often as they might.

After a brainstorming session at one of my seminars, the managers of VNA hammered out a list of its competitive advantages—or at least what the managers thought were competitive advantages. At the top of the list was the association's nonprofit status. Surely, they thought, that had to count heavily with doctors and patients. Wouldn't you assume a nonprofit organization would cost less than one that is run for profit? Wouldn't that be a critical competitive advantage?

Some weeks after the seminar, my firm designed and commissioned the customer research. We surveyed two target markets: doctors in private practice and managers of assisted-living facilities. Our goal was to determine what criteria each used when making "referring decisions." Note: The surveys for each target market were not identical. Nor were the competitive advantages cited identical. Each market has different buying criteria and must be dealt with separately, so we created two lists of competitive advantages and conducted two different surveys. When you use the same list of competitive advantages for all your target markets, a dangerous disparity can emerge. What is important to a doctor, for example, might not matter so much to the manager of an assisted-living facility.

When the research was completed, I scheduled a meeting with the same VNA staff that attended the workshop a couple months earlier. I gave everyone two sheets of paper. One listed the top fifteen competitive advantages that we tested with managers of assisted-living facilities. The second sheet listed the fifteen different attributes that we tested with doctors as described on page 143. I asked the group to indicate on the sheets which competitive advantages the doctors and the managers rated first, second, and third in their buying decisions. I also asked them to write an "L" next to three things that they thought would rank least important.

We soon discovered that dangerous disparity was rearing its ugly head. The staff members were way off in guessing which attributes were most important to each market. In fact, the attribute that won the most votes for first place in the doctor survey was rated only fifth by the staff. The attribute that won the most votes for managers of assisted-living facilities was rated ninth out of fifteen. Topping the list of *least important* attributes on both surveys was—you guessed it—not-for-profit status. The staff's top pick mattered not a whit to customers.

As a result, VNA stopped touting its nonprofit status and instead stressed the competitive advantages that their customers cared most about. In VNA's marketing campaign, there is nary a mention of their nonprofit status. Instead, they simply mention these points verified by industry watchdogs:

- Patients cared for by VNA are rehospitalized 23 percent less than the competition.
- Patients visited by VNA staff require emergency room treatment 34 percent less often than patients of competitors.
- VNA's incidence of unexpected deaths is 47 percent lower than the national average.
- VNA's patients improve 34 percent faster than the national average.
- VNA discharges patients only when at-home care is no longer required.
- Patient satisfaction with VNA services is 99 percent.

VNA's traffic started to increase almost immediately after it began the new marketing campaign touting its competitive advantages. Don Crow, the CEO, told me that six months after the workshop, VNA broke company records by increasing its revenues 40 percent that year—and revenues continue to rise.

What's especially notable here is that the increase in business can be attributed almost solely to VNA's newly minted competitive advantages and competitive positioning statements. The organization doesn't employ traditional salespeople, so its "selling" is done by nurses and customer-service people. VNA simply arms them with its lists of competitive advantages while continuing to advertise them in print. I have turned CPAs, interior designers, and nurses into sales closers without a single day of sales training.

A BLOCKBUSTER CASE OF DANGEROUS DISPARITY

For a glaring example of dangerous disparity, look no farther than your local Blockbuster outlet. The movie-rental chain had once been highly profitable when it enjoyed substantial competitive advantages that trumped the competition. In its early days, Blockbuster set out to become the category killer in the marketplace, and it succeeded. Since its stores had much more inventory and better pricing than those of mom-and-pop and small-chain rivals, competitors faded. Blockbuster became the world's largest movie-rental chain, with about 9,100 company-owned or franchised stores in 25 countries (about 65 percent are in the United States). The company rents more than 1 billion videos, DVDs, and video games at its Blockbuster Video outlets each year.

As Blockbuster grew, it began to enjoy economies of scale, more leverage with suppliers, and more widespread brand recognition. For many Americans, the giant chain was the only place in town for rentals. They liked Blockbuster's broad selection of movies and the frequency of new releases. But they certainly didn't like the late fees. Customers were quick to rent movies, on tape or DVD, but they were not always prompt at returning them. And they had to pay for their tardiness—sometimes even more than the rental fee. Of course, customers had only themselves to blame, but they still felt cheated.

Late fees were a headache for customers but a bonanza for Blockbuster. They accounted for some $300 million a year in revenues. That princely sum came right out of customers' pockets, just for returning movies a day or so late. Adding to the discontent was Blockbuster's confusing policy about when late fees kicked in. For movies labeled "Two-Day Rental," the late-fee meter started at noon on the third day after rental, frustrating customers who preferred to drop off their movies later in the day.

By late 2004, things were not so rosy for Blockbuster. Rentals began to slow as customers increasingly began watching movies on cable or pay-per-view TV, or by purchasing them outright. Customers were making fewer trips to the video store. And, whenever they did, they still had to contend with those annoying late fees.

Even as its market growth was slowing, Blockbuster, which had been recently spun off from giant Viacom, had trouble on another front. Online competition from Wal-Mart and Netflix offered something Blockbuster didn't—no late fees. With Netflix, for $17.99 a month, customers can rent as many movies as they like by mail, in batches of three, without any shipping or late fees. In order to receive more DVDs, you simply have to first return the ones you have.

Netflix—which eventually bought out the Wal-Mart venture—suddenly had a strong competitive advantage over Blockbuster: no late fees. It became clear to Blockbuster management that, as painful as the move was, it, too, had to eliminate late fees. Competitive disadvantages must be dealt with quickly, and Blockbuster knew it.

But here is where the story gets screwy. Blockbuster assumed that its customers would be thrilled to escape late fees. So thrilled, in fact, that they wouldn't mind a few conditions. With great fanfare, Blockbuster unveiled its new policy with a TV ad blitz: "No late fees—ever." The ads didn't make much mention of the strings attached.

But the strings mattered. In fact, they got Blockbuster in a lot of hot water, not only with their customers but also with attorneys general in all fifty states and the District of Columbia. "No late fees—ever" was an oversimplification. If you keep a Blockbuster video for more than seven days, you could wind up being billed for the purchase of the video. Blockbuster "assumed" anyone keeping a video beyond seven days *wanted* to buy it. The cost—minus the rental fee—is automatically deducted from your credit card. If you return the movie after seven days, you aren't charged for the purchase of the movie but still have to pay another $1.25 restocking fee.

Blockbuster's new policy promised to give customers a free ride for turning in movies a few days late. But instead it brought howls of protest from customers and the media, as well as a raft of lawsuits charging deceptive advertising. What had originally been conceived as a big concession to customers had blown up in Blockbuster's face.

The giant chain made two classic blunders: It misjudged its customers, and it overstated its case. I can't help but wonder what customer research Blockbuster did before rolling out that misleading ad campaign. Dangerous disparity coupled with deceptive advertising equals disaster. Blockbuster wound up paying $630,000 to settle claims brought by forty-seven states and the District of Columbia, and three more suits from New Jersey, Vermont, and New Hampshire are still pending. The company also had to give refunds to customers who claimed the ads led them to believe they could rent the movies for as long as they liked at no additional cost.

As I see it, Blockbuster could have avoided this entire mess if it had accurately read its customers. A few thousand dollars' worth of good research could have saved them the big settlement fees and maybe even brought forth some solid ideas to replace this bad one. Blockbuster might have realized it had become a company you love to hate—in no small part because its late fees serve as a living reminder of how disorganized you are, unable to even return movies on time. You never want your customers to feel badly about themselves after using your products.

In an earlier chapter, I talked about the shadow effect. Airlines found that if planes were late, passengers rated everything else about the carriers poorly. Blockbuster's long-term policy of late fees, as well as some other dubious promotions over the years, had overshadowed any goodwill its customers may have had toward the company. They felt they were being ripped off and anticipated that whatever Blockbuster did about late fees would amount to a scam. It didn't matter that customers were indeed getting a big break—up to a week's rental instead of a few days. Nor did they appreciate that they would be notified twice by phone and once by mail before being charged full price for the video, and could *still* return it for a $1.25 restocking fee. Indeed, Blockbuster reported that 96 percent of customers returned movies within the seven-day grace period. Nonetheless, the new policy was perceived as a rip-off, and the misleading ads only fueled the flames. Customers bashed the company, the media followed, and there were even calls for groups to boycott Blockbuster. "There are thousands of Blockbuster locations in Black neighborhoods," commented Dante Lee, founder of

BlackNews.com, "and we're encouraging African-Americans to stay away from the company."

Blockbuster is now fighting Netflix on its own turf, with its own online service that offers movies for as little as $14.99 per month. There are no late fees, but you pay a monthly fee, regardless of the number of rentals you order and receive by mail. Blockbuster has a massive investment in its outlets, and that is still where most of its revenues come from. Yet its walk-in customers are now very leery of any claims the company makes. If they were unhappy about late fees before, they are bitter now—not a great climate for growth. In fact, what used to be the Blockbuster store in my neighborhood is now a Chinese restaurant.

HOW TO READ YOUR CUSTOMERS ACCURATELY

The late Peter Drucker, the noted management guru, wrote in the *Wall Street Journal* that "customer research may be more important than market research—but far more difficult."

I'll drink to that. Market research tells you where the market is headed, how big it is, how big your slice of the pie is, and what trends are developing. It is an important gauge of the field of competition. But customer research is even more important. You cannot afford to make assumptions about your customers' preferences.

Of course, it's easy to shoot first and never ask any questions of customers; entrepreneurs do it all the time. And it's a dumb mistake.

I always ask my CEO groups, "How many of you rely on relationships for your business?" About 80 percent raise their hands. Relationships are important. But they can be fleeting. They can also cause you to read your customers wrong.

Have you ever had this kind of experience? You are on the golf course with one of your good customers, who has been a little tense all game. As you approach the eighteenth hole, you find out why. He's been waiting for the right moment to launch into the kiss-off: "You're not going to like this, Harry. I know we've been buying from you for years, but we're in a budget crunch. XYZ, Inc., just offered us a heck of a deal and, well, you know, we gotta go where the best deal is these days. Better prices. I've got to move the account from you. So sorry. Let's get a beer. "

You are floored. You thought you knew your customer well, and that he was happy doing business with you. You were sure that he was telling you everything you needed to know to keep him happy. But he wasn't telling what was *really* on his mind—that he thinks you're charging too much and he can get a cheaper deal elsewhere. You have let yourself be defeated on *price*.

I used to deliver a presentation on market research for middle-market companies called "Look Before You Leap." It had three basic messages:

- Entrepreneurs think they know their customers so well that customer research is not necessary. That's one reason so many of them fail.

- Relationship customers don't tell you the truth when you ask them face-to-face, "Is there anything wrong?" Instead, they usually act like adulterers being questioned by their spouses: "I haven't been pulling away—it's just the stress of the office, honey." If the truth will hurt, your friendly customers will lie to you rather than upset you.

- They will always tell you price is the tiebreaker. Congratulations, you have allowed yourself to become a commodity! Hope you enjoyed the game; too bad you took your eye off the ball.

As Drucker said, customer research is difficult—far more difficult than market research—but much more important, in my opinion. Example: Suppose you are launching a new product—a new type of toothbrush, for example. Your market-research folks try it out on focus groups, and they love it. The results from every demographic are great, and the competition lacks your advantage—*your toothbrush never wears out.*

You go to market, and sales take off for six months. Then they slow down. Your eternal but expensive toothbrush is no longer flying off the shelves. Why? Perhaps only a few consumers are willing to spend the difference in price for your toothbrush—and they created the initial flurry of sales. Or perhaps consumers didn't like the packaging or the design of the product, one they would have to live with a long time. Or maybe they just liked buying different-colored brushes once in a while and enjoyed the tingle of brand-new brushes. Only persistent consumer research would have revealed the real reason. Asking the tough questions of customers familiar with your product is the only way of finding out the truth. Prelaunch groups can't do that.

Gillette is a sterling example of a company that not only innovates with technology but also heeds its customer research. When Jacob Schick brought out the first electric razor a millennium or so ago (so it seems), it was like the eternal toothbrush. Much more expensive than a razor and blades, but all you had to do was plug it in and it would work for years. Gillette could have panicked and launched its own line of electric razors, but instead it listened to its customers. Gillette learned that for a lot of reasons, a lot of shavers didn't like electric razors. Gillette listened. For decades, it has kept on giving its customers what they want—closer and closer nick-free shaves, one micromillimeter at a time.

DON'T TRY THIS AT HOME

Good customer research is difficult because you must use an outside firm that does not identify your company when performing its interviews. Otherwise, you won't get honest results. If you do a survey yourself and identify who you are, customers won't give you straight answers. Even if you try to conceal your identity, the voices of your employees making the calls may be recognizable. Or your employees might inadvertently slip.

It's essential that the caller remain anonymous. Studies have shown that when a participant in the survey doesn't know who is calling, the topic of price is rarely among the top three buying criteria. But when the participant knows the caller's company, price is almost always first. With you, the customer is negotiating every step of the way. With you, he wants a deal. But with an outsider, he will tell the truth.

Moral: Hire a good consumer-research firm to do your surveying. Don't just select a firm on price—remember, price is not a differentiator. Ask to see previous survey results and pay attention to how the questionnaires are framed. Good firms prepare your questionnaire, which is a science and a tricky task to accomplish on your own. But it is vital to getting solid results. Stay away from those fill-in-the-blanks questionnaires people are peddling over the Internet. One size doesn't fit all. Your questionnaire should be custom-made.

In fact, a lousy questionnaire can defeat the whole purpose of your survey. I recently got a call from a CEO who had heard one of my presentations on competitive advantage. He was proud to tell me that he had gone through the workshop exercise and come up with a list of his company's competitive advantages, which he then proceeded to vet with his customers. But instead of hiring a good research firm to help him with his questionnaire, he used one of the boilerplate surveys he got off the Internet. He asked if he could forward the results to me for comment.

After I saw what he had sent, I had no comment. I was, in fact, speechless. All I could do was ask him what conclusions he could draw from it. The survey only allowed customers to make note of what they wanted: A+ standards for delivery, customer service, turnaround time, product availability, and so on. But because there was no section to evaluate their current vendor's offerings, the survey was worthless.

FIND OUT WHAT YOUR CUSTOMERS
REALLY WANT

When was the last time your organization hired an outside firm to do *customer* research? What has kept you from doing so?

If you were to hire out, what would be the objective of your study? (It is best to have one clear objective per study.) When companies try to extract too much information, the findings are often muddy.

How often do you meet internally to discuss your competitive advantages and how they rate with your customers? Add this to your calendar for quarterly review, at a minimum. Better yet, do it monthly.

Do you have someone in your company in charge of this important discipline? Large companies often have market research managers who act as a liaison with research firms. If you are a middle-market company, do you have someone to whom you can assign this responsibility? If not, hire someone. The return on investment will be outstanding.

CHAPTER 8

Identifying Your Own Company's Competitive Advantages
The Devil Is in the Details

YOUR COMPETITIVE ADVANTAGE MAY LIE IN THE product or service you provide, if it is clearly superior to the competition. If so, you're lucky. But chances are that is not the case. Too many companies spend too much time and money trying to convince customers that their products or services are really "better" than the other guys', when they really aren't. For too long, Miller Brewing Co.'s slogan for its Lite beer was "tastes great, less filling." But to beer drinkers, Coors Light and Bud Light and Amstel Light and other light-beer brands also "taste great" and are "less filling." Miller was promoting light beer—not Lite beer.

Customers want to know in concrete terms what it is about your product or service that is better than the rest. Consider my client Southeastern Printing. The lithographic printing company offers complete electronic pre-press services, sophisticated computer-to-plate systems, and today's most advanced Heidelberg presses.

Printing might seem to be as close to a commodity business as you can get. Customers expect that their printing jobs will be finished accurately and on time. In fact, they insist on it. Like the passengers on Southwest Airlines, what's most important to them is getting the job done right and on time.

But "stuff" happens. Sometimes printers foul up, sometimes customers cause problems that result in delays. At our workshop session on competitive advantage, I asked SEP managers what the company does to assure printing accuracy and job completion by deadline. They told me that they had a ten-point quality check for all print jobs. It was developed over the years to make sure SEP avoided critical mistakes. I got the impression this ten-point quality check was as important to SEP as a pilot's checklist before taking off.

"Really? Do you tell your customers about your checklist?" I asked. The reply was "Well, no, we just do it to make sure every job goes out accurately."

I cringed, but I wasn't surprised that SEP failed to let its customers know the details of its quality control. Good companies often follow tight internal procedures to assure quality control and on-time delivery of their products or services, yet fail to let customers know what they are. There seems to be a reluctance to let customers know what goes on inside the company's walls, even if doing so would benefit the company. We are not talking sausages or law here—the making of which no one prefers to see. We're talking printing. SEP has a very high rate of accurate completions because it takes extra steps to ensure it.

If XYZ printer tells you, "We deliver accurate print jobs on schedule," and SEP says, "We deliver on time because 95 percent of print jobs are completed in-house and all undergo a ten-point quality check," who is most likely to get your order?

During the SEP workshop session, we continued drilling down for other attributes of SEP that were likely to impress customers but that weren't being broadcast. We came up with an interesting list of advantages and competitive positioning statements, many of which I suggest you think about adapting for your own business:

- SEP is in the top 1 percent of printers in the United States.
- SEP invested $10 million in new technology that cuts job time in half and speeds delivery of the job to the bindery.
- Ninety-five percent of digital proofs are ready in twenty-four hours.
- Our own fleet of trucks services six counties.
- We're environmentally friendly. SEP recycles its waste.

- SEP is the only area printing company that can print up to ten colors at one time.
- Ninety percent of our business comes from referral.

Like my client Southeastern Printing, you too might find an edge in educating your customers about what they are getting for their money. Give them some details to chew on. Even if your product or service isn't special by itself, the way you make it, test it, package it, deliver it, as well as other extras you provide, can make the critical difference in customers' buying decisions.

One company I worked with, ABB Optical, distributes contact lenses nationwide. Again, there would seem to be little that ABB could do to differentiate itself on the basis of product alone. After all, there are plenty of distributors selling the same contact lenses. So it began asking questions of its clients, including eye doctors and specialists, to find out what it could do to make their lives easier. Buyers complained that the typical ordering process was confusing and time-consuming, especially when dealing with different suppliers. ABB went to work simplifying the whole ordering process, which turned out to be very difficult for them but very beneficial for customers.

While competitors were working on the front end (their Web sites), ABB set about getting the back of the house in order by automating the warehouse. It built a technology platform for a commodity product. Anyone can sell contact lenses, but ABB is now the largest provider of online services for suppliers like Sears, LensCrafters,

Ifinity, Visionworld, Pearl, and others. They can all place their orders for their customers on ABB's Web site.

Also, while competitors were wooing eye doctors to buy their stuff, ABB was busy devising an online ordering system that would make life easier for doctors. Patients can do their own ordering. So if you are a patient of Dr. Jones and use his Web site for ordering more lenses, you may think you are ordering from Dr. Jones. But you are in the ABB system. And Dr. Jones doesn't have to deal with any of the paperwork or other details. This logistical advantage allowed ABB to blow away the competition.

ABB now cites these competitive advantages:

- One phone call or fax to place an order
- One package to process instead of several from different lensmakers
- One place to exchange or return products
- One monthly statement
- Immediate notification of product availability
- E-mail notification of product shipment
- Direct ship to patient
- Orders can be placed Mon. to Fri. from 8:00 A.M. to 9:00 P.M.
- Forty-eight hour delivery on most orders
- Online ordering 24/7

Since implementing the streamlined ordering process, ABB has grown far faster than the overall market for contact lenses. In fact, the company has grown from $30 million to $120 million in annual revenues over the past five years. Much of that growth came through acquisitions, as ABB snatched up several slow-footed competitors who failed to address their customers' needs the way that ABB did.

IS AN EDUCATED CONSUMER YOUR BEST CUSTOMER?

It is a source of great frustration for many a marketing executive: competing with a superior, pricier product when your customers don't know why it is superior, or simply don't believe your claims. Consumers have been conditioned to distrust a lot of consumer advertising. You won't win the "quality" fight with advertising blather.

Shirtmaker Ike Behar considers himself a craftsman first, and many would agree. *Menswear* magazine wrote of him: "What makes Ike Behar different from other shirt makers is a near fanatic devotion to craftsmanship."

But "craftsmanship" is a tough sell. It's too general and too shopworn a term. Would-be buyers are not going to spend $150 or so on a shirt because of its "superior craftsmanship" unless they have proof it is worth it. Behar decided that he would tell shoppers exactly what makes his shirts worth the premium price—and give them an education in the process. In his advertising, Behar describes his shirts the way a watchmaker might tick off all the features of a fine timepiece. Here are his nine reasons for buying an Ike Behar shirt:

- The exclusive, patented Diamond Quilted Collar. The quilting process provides the extra strength needed for the most utilized part of each shirt: the collar. It reinforces the European lining, which adds to the performance of the collar, preventing the lining from shifting and shrinking.
- Single-needle stitching. This provides each seam with twice the strength of a standard seam. The process takes three times longer than conventional methods, but the resulting seam is flatter, more comfortable, and more durable.
- Tight stitching. The detail in an Ike Behar shirt can be seen in the eighteen to twenty-two stitches per inch used throughout the shirt. More stitches per inch provide a neater, flatter, stronger seam.
- Handkerchief-rolled seams. This tailoring technique prevents puckering and produces an elegantly finished shirt, with added durability.
- Buttons. We carefully match our buttons—ranging from mother-of-pearl to unbreakable plastic—to complement the fabric and style of each shirt. A spare button is sewn on the front tail of every shirt.
- High-count fabrics. We use the finest Egyptian cottons, provided by the same mills that supply Loro Piana, Zegna, Lorenzini, Armani, and several other luxury brands. We have established solid relationships with

our partners overseas to guarantee fabric exclusivity.

- There are fifty-two steps involved in making an Ike Behar shirt. Each shirt sports an authentic split yoke, removable collar stays, and button sleeve placket.
- Guarantee. "Ike Behar stands 100 percent behind every shirt he makes." If you are unhappy with the shirt, bring it back to the retailer.
- Neckwear. The fabrics we use in our ties are woven of 100 percent Italian silk. Each tie is hand-tailored.

I love using Behar's list in my seminars on competitive advantage, because he so brilliantly articulates the reasons why you should buy his shirts. But it's not simply the wordsmithing that matters. It's the facts. He supplies the kinds of details and education that fussy shirt buyers relish and that newbies love to absorb. He makes you want to run out to the nearest Saks, Neiman Marcus, or Nordstrom to buy a shirt or three.

The old adage about an educated consumer being the best customer still rings true for Ike Behar. On Wall Street—where dress shirts, not suits, now make the man—young bankers and brokers can now tell you all about Egyptian cotton and hand-finished collars. They get a lot of that information from Ike Behar, and that's why they wear his shirts. As we say in my workshops, "If you do something special, explain it to your customers. Give them specific reasons for paying more for your product or service." Don't just say you deliver quality; spell it out like Ike does.

Tilley Hats uses a strategy similar to Behar's in selling

its high-quality sun hats. Tilley hats actually come with instructions on their construction, care, and use. You're even told the degree of sun protection the hat offers. Customers lap it up, especially the yachtsmen, who are an important target market.

IT'S NOT ONLY WHAT YOU DO, BUT HOW YOU DO IT

As we've said, your competitive advantage may lie not in the products or services themselves, but in how you provide them. It could lie in the terms you give your clients—the guarantees, inventory, financial terms, packaging, volume, and delivery.

You might be able to provide just-in-time delivery, for example, saving your customers warehousing and other costs. You may have information in your database to share with customers to help them turn over their inventories faster. You might provide valuable employee training or market information.

To stir your thinking a bit, here is a sample list of deliverables that you can measure against your competition in order to arrive at competitive advantages for your company. (Your own company's deliverables will probably differ somewhat, but you'll get the idea.)

- Product knowledge
- Post-sale tech support

- Inventory availability
- Product performance
- Tech-savvy reps
- Consistently complete shipments
- Good delivery condition
- Easy installation
- Fast response to customer queries
- Superior communications
- Unique design
- Installation training
- Shipping documents
- Sales leads
- Product training

Training is one area that many companies overlook in compiling their competitive advantages. I always ask clients, "Do you provide training for your customers? Do you provide training for your employees?" Many do, but few say anything about it.

HornerXpress is a worldwide distributor of swimming pool chemicals and equipment. But it does more than ship products to pool-service companies and other retailers. HornerXpress realizes that in order to grow and prosper, its customers have to grow and prosper first. To help them avoid the pitfalls that doom many small businesses, HornerXpress provides courses in basic accounting, accounts receivable, and marketing, in addition to training on the company's products. By making such training a cornerstone of its "win-win" philosophy, the company has seen revenues grow from $30 million in 1990 to $160 million in 2005 and now boasts customers in more than ninety countries.

Your own employee training can also yield competitive advantages, if it is directed at the customer. Some companies don't allow their drivers or customer-service people on the job without spending a lot of time in the classroom first. If you do similar training, tell your customers about it. Your statements might sound like this: "We invest over X dollars each year training our employees to serve you better."

Once again, tell 'em what you do, tell 'em why, and tell 'em what it costs. Let them know exactly what they are getting for their money so that the competitor can't lure them away with a few price points.

COUNTING THE CALORIES AND CARBS

The fast-food industry had recently found itself in the crosshairs of health and nutrition specialists who blame the industry for peddling extra fat and calories to unwitting consumers. The giant fast-food chains have even been taken to court for fattening up their customers. (The suits have been dismissed so far.)

To satisfy the health police, most chains have begun putting less-fattening items on their menus. McDonald's, for example, added salads, apple slices, and other seemingly leaner fare to its burgers and fries. (Yet its new salads could contain more calories and carbs than its burgers, depending on the type and amount of the dressing that is added.)

Ruby Tuesday followed suit and began offering lower-carb dishes. But like McDonald's and other chains, it was fully aware that most of their customers chose to ignore the more slimming fare. They still wanted their burgers, fries, and fried chicken, despite the health police. Those are the items that move.

Ruby Tuesday decided that all their customers should know the score and make their own decisions. The chains now tells diners exactly how many calories, fat, grams, net carbs, and fiber are contained in all 110 food items on its menu. The weight-conscious can measure their meals to the last carb and calorie, while other customers can chow down in peace.

It didn't take much effort for Ruby Tuesday to digitize the nutritional value of its food items, but Ruby Tuesday was alone in doing it and thereby gained a competitive advantage. If your spouse is watching her or his diet and you and the kids crave a fast-food fix, where would you go?

Note: McDonald's is now breaking down the nutritional content of its menu. Better late than never, but Ruby Tuesday has already stolen the thunder.

WHAT DOESN'T SHOW CAN ALSO MEAN A LOT

Like the earlier example of Southeastern Printing, your company might have some strong *internal* competitive advantages that your customers don't see, but which can and should influence their buying decisions. Here are a few:

Buying power. If you do a high volume of business, or hold exclusive franchises on certain products, you obviously have clout with your suppliers. Buying in volume not only means lower costs for your customer, it can mean speedier deliveries, special deliveries of unusually large or small quantities, and better service if anything goes wrong. It can also be a feather in your cap if a large manufacturer with an admired brand chooses you to sell its wares. So let your customers know about your brand-name suppliers.

Substitute products and services. The CEO of an advertising agency, was about to lose a key client—not because the agency was doing a poor job in ad creation and placement, but because the client wanted to make a big splash with a direct-mail campaign. What the client didn't know was that the agency had a relationship with another ad agency that specialized in direct-mail campaigns for banks, insurance companies, publications, and other clients. Unaware of the connection between the two agencies, the client assumed he would have to go elsewhere for help with the direct-mail campaign. In the end, he didn't move the account after all, once he discovered that the original agency could handle the job through the affiliated agency. But the agency learned a lesson. He now makes sure all his clients know all the services that can be arranged through his agency.

Market position. There is security in numbers, and if a potential customer knows that your company dominates its market, he or she is likely to feel more comfortable dealing with you. There is a good reason you're on top—satisfied customers. Your market position doesn't have to be national to be impressive. If you are the biggest in your own region or county, for example, that can boost your credibility, whether you are a realtor, a law firm, a beer distributor, or a hospital. Don't be shy about it.

Experience. Your customers probably don't give a hoot about when your company was founded, but few would like to be pioneers with a company going through its learning curve. More important than when you opened shop is the expertise you bring to the game. If you have a staff of engineers with an average of fifteen years' experience, or if they hold patents or have won awards, make sure your clients know it. Your competitors surely do.

Production advantages. If you've invested in the latest equipment, have better access to materials, or boast a heftier inventory, let your customers know. And, as always, look for impressive metrics to back it up. "We can turn around jobs a third faster than our nearest competitor," for example. Or "We just invested $2 million in the latest manufacturing technology, which allows us to double production output, shortening your delivery time by 50 percent."

More often than not, a company will say something like "We just invested in the latest manufacturing technology in the industry." That's a good start, but next you should simply answer the "So what?" question. What does that technology mean to your customer?

Distribution advantages. If you are a supplier, perhaps the physical location of your warehouses or the size of your truck fleet gives you an edge in receiving and shipping materials and products. This can translate into faster order fulfillment. Find out exactly how much faster, and let your customers know. Similarly, if you buy goods wholesale and sell retail, and have more distribution outlets than the competition, specify the number. ABB Optical, the company I introduced earlier in the chapter, has acquired companies in California, New York, and Massachusetts to ensure quicker delivery around the country.

Government relations. Uncle Sam can stick his nose into your business and your customers' businesses in numerous ways. If you are in the construction business, for example, you might run afoul of zoning and environmental regulations that threaten your customers' projects. If you run a high-tech company, you might have to deal with patent issues. If you manufacture products that could be dangerous if misused—from ladders to fertilizer to guns—then you are no stranger to lobbying and litigation. Experience in dealing with the various layers of government and its labyrinth of laws and regulations doesn't come easily. Your customers can benefit from both the results of your experience and the relevant knowledge you can pass along to them.

The list of advantages goes on, depending on the business that you are in. The point is to give your customers confidence that they are in good, responsible hands when dealing with you. Your goal should be to remove or minimize their concerns about risk of buying. Your competitive advantages and competitive positioning statements can help put them at ease.

COMPETITIVE ADVANTAGES
THAT REALLY DELIVER

Your competitive advantage may lie in the "fine print" surrounding your product or service—warranties or guarantees, for example. Or it could be in how you deliver that product or service to your customer— salmon that is always freshly smoked, for example.

Make a list of every one of your deliverables. The list could include such things as technical support after sale; responsiveness of company personnel to problems; instructions that are easy to read and follow; new-product designs and packaging to meet contemporary needs; precise shipping and inventory information; consistent on-time delivery; easy access to key personnel in case of problems, and so on.

Do you measure your deliverables? Which deliverables are you not measuring today that could translate into competitive advantages or competitive positioning statements for your prospects and customers?

Do you have any idea what the competition measures and brags about? If not, red alert! If you don't know what they are touting, you won't know where you stand.

How do you hold your staff accountable for each function? Does your company value the deliverables that are important to your customer? How do you know?

Make sure everyone at your company understands his or her role in creating or supporting competitive advantages within the organization and has a chance to pipe up.

If you can provide your customers with necessary training that is otherwise very expensive or difficult to arrange, you could have a killer competitive advantage on your hands.

What operational decisions might you need to make to ensure that competitive advantages are alive and well in your organization? Do you need to streamline a process or invest in new equipment or specialists? Should you consider making an acquisition? Competitive advantages don't just happen. They are conscious, well-planned decisions, executed superbly.

CHAPTER 9

If You Don't Have a Competitive Advantage, Create One

YOU MAY FIND THAT YOUR COMPANY REALLY DOESN'T have any eye-popping competitive advantages. If so, I'll show you how to create some. Creating competitive advantages can not only save your company; doing so could turn around your business and give it new focus for years to come. Warning: You might have to make some expensive and time-consuming changes in the way you are conducting your business. On the other hand, you may be able to create some competitive advantages without investing anything but a little sweat equity. Whatever they are, competitive advantages don't come out of the blue; they are the result of conscious strategic decisions and operational changes based on competitive analysis and customer research. But no one ever said that running a business was easy. (After all, the key word is *running*. If you stand still, you'll get run over by the guys behind you.)

I've worked with some CEOs who were quick to see the need for their companies to develop competitive advantages, but after identifying what had to be done, they failed to follow through.

It breaks my heart to see enthusiasm morph into lethargy as weeks turn into months and years with nothing done, as ideas and strategies die on the vine. In one case, a marketing director resigned just as customer research was about to commence. The new director was reluctant to follow through until he had tried out a few marketing ideas of his own. Months went by, the research was never conducted, the new marketing director left, and the project remains in limbo.

If you are a CEO, business owner, or senior executive, you have to make it clear to all your employees that you are committed to developing competitive advantages and will stay committed. Identifying your competitive advantage is not a one-time exercise. You should discuss your advantages with your staff at least once a quarter and make them the basis for any strategic planning exercises you conduct.

When I first met Beverly Raphael, she was an accidental CEO. Her husband Richard had run a construction business, RCC Associates, which specialized in the interior design and construction of high-end retail stores and restaurants. A few short months after I began working with Richard, he was diagnosed with multiple brain tumors. When he died four months later, Beverly found herself responsible for the business he had started twenty-eight years earlier.

Beverly was no stranger to the business world. For fifteen years she had owned and operated a firm that represented sellers of women's apparel, with clients throughout the Southeast. But construction was not a field in which she felt comfortable. After Richard was diagnosed with his illness, in an effort to plan ahead, he promoted two long-term employees to president and executive vice president. They were ready to step up to the plate but lacked the skills to fill Richard's shoes. RCC was doing OK, but Beverly knew from her own business experience that OK was not good enough. It was only a matter of time before the lack of sales and poor management would have a severe effect on the life of the business.

RCC had been ignoring what was happening in the industry. The boom in new construction had brought lots of new competitors to town, many of whom were cutting corners to offer lower bids. Competitors were exaggerating what they could deliver. RCC didn't do business by making false promises and had no intention of changing its stripes. Its integrity was what had won it plenty of big accounts and a lot of repeat business. But RCC wasn't landing enough new clients. The new president lacked the contacts and relationships that Richard had built. After the founder's death, the company took for granted one of its most important clients, a high-end shopping mall in which RCC had been the contractor of choice for more than fifty projects. Because RCC was unable to give the mall manager the attention he was accustomed to, he began referring new tenants to another contractor.

There aren't a lot of widows who would do what Beverly then did: She fired the president and took charge of the company herself. She knew she had to foster the relationships and build on the reputation that her husband had worked so hard to earn. She began calling and visiting clients, reestablishing ties. About eighteen months later, RCC signed up for my competitive advantage workshop. They wanted a compelling reason for people to choose RCC.

We scheduled the workshop for a Saturday. Beverly heard lots of moans and groans from staff about giving up a treasured weekend day. Project managers and field people who rarely got involved in corporate decisions had no idea what this "competitive advantage" thing was all about and would rather have been out fishing.

But once I explained what competitive advantage was all about, their creative juices started flowing. RCC managers pointed to a number of competitive advantages, including referral rates, repeat business from top national chains, cost savings from preconstruction engineering, 24/7 customer service, and an impressive list of high-profile clients, including The Cheesecake Factory, Louis Vuitton, Tiffany, Prada, Hermès, Gucci, Chanel, and Neiman Marcus.

By the end of the day, we had an impressive list of competitive advantages, and the RCC staffers were pumped. Instead of bolting out of the room and onto the golf course, most hung around. They felt they had just learned a great deal about their own company and were eager to spread the word about its competitive advantages. They even asked Beverly if they could plan another session for the employees who weren't able to attend.

I had to tell them that their job wasn't finished, however. I reminded them about dangerous disparity and the need to run their competitive advantages by their customers. They followed my advice, and we hired an independent research company to survey prospects and clients and ask them to rate what mattered most to them when choosing a construction firm. The prospects and clients were unaware that RCC had commissioned the research.

Once the customer research findings were in, I met with Beverly and the RCC staff to assess the results. I provided them with the list of fifteen attributes that we tested. I asked them to guess which three were rated first, second, and third. I also asked them to indicate with an "L" the three attributes that they thought RCC customers would find least important. RCC was no different from any other company I have worked with. Only a few people even came close to guessing which items were most and least important.

Most employees thought that RCC's list of high-profile clients like Tiffany and Gucci and The Cheesecake Factory would score heavily with customers. But glitz was far less important than the nitty-gritty. Customers said that the most desirable attribute of a construction company was the timely completion of the punch list. When a project is completed, the customer and the construction manager make up a punch list—issues that remain unresolved at the end of a project. Retailers and restaurateurs lose money when their stores don't open on time, and a long punch list is often seen as the culprit. RCC's survey revealed that timely completion of a project makes or breaks the customer's experience. It has a shadow effect on the whole job. If a construction company does everything right but doesn't finish on time or is still "fixing" things after the store opens, then even an A+ job gets a C−.

So RCC created a competitive advantage by attacking that punch list. It began telling prospective clients that RCC aimed at having no punch list at all when a project was completed. "Our common goal is to have you open, happy and making money on or before the scheduled turnover," read the literature. "RCC strives to complete each project 'punch list free.'" This was a bold move, as clients themselves often request last-minute changes that throw contractors off schedule. But RCC's goal was stated: No Punch List. It has become RCC's mantra, and customers love it. Annual revenues have doubled from $34 million when Beverly called me to set up the workshop, to $68 million just two years later.

IT ALL STARTS WITH THE BEAN

John Scharffenberger didn't need to do any customer research to know what would make his dark chocolate products sell better. As a maker of premium chocolate in small batches "from bean to bar," he was only too aware of a critical limitation: He couldn't get his hands on enough high-quality cacao beans. He had to go to middlemen for 80 percent of the cacao he needed, and he could never be sure of the quality of what he was buying. To his suppliers, cacao was a commodity. To Scharffenberger, it was his livelihood.

Try as he might, with his relative small size, he lacked the leverage to get the quality beans he needed to make his premium products, including dark chocolate-covered ginger and espresso beans. So he decided to go to the source. As reported in *Fast Company* magazine, he packed his bags and went off to Central America to find the best organic cacao he could.

It took nearly a year for him to find and sign up cacao farmers in the Dominican Republic, Guatemala, and Colombia who were willing to adopt organic growth methods and sign contracts with him. Some farmers were Quiche Indians in remote Guatemala, who live near the source of the original cacao trees. In the Dominican Republic, he also wound up helping to save the rain forest by hiring farmers to grow cacao instead of clearing the forest understory for cattle grazing.

Scharffen Berger Chocolate Maker generates about $10 million a year and has excellent growth prospects now that it is assured a supply of high-quality, organically grown beans. That is the company's competitive advantage, and it didn't come easily. But that means it can't be duplicated easily, either. *Fast Company* cited the company as one of its Fast 50 Winners of 2005.

OF ORANGES AND AIRPORTS

Glades Crop Care provides agricultural consulting to fruit and vegetable growers by helping farmers boost their crops. It is recognized as one of the best consultancies in the business. A few years ago, executives at Glades learned that the federal and state governments were seeking bids to create a fresh produce safety program for growers. Normally, universities are the recipients of such government contracts. But Glades decided it would enter the bidding. Although food safety wasn't its basic business, Glades knew that its customers—farmers—would soon be taking food safety very seriously.

The law does not require food-safety programs for fresh produce, as it does for meat, poultry, seafood, and juice. But Glades saw the handwriting on the wall. Many produce buyers, including supermarket and restaurant chains, had already begun to demand that the growers who supply them institute food-safety programs. While the farmers were reluctant to invest the time and money needed to implement these programs, their biggest customers persisted. Farmers were in need of food-safety programs, and Glades saw a unique opportunity to help them while helping itself.

First, it had to win the $500,000 government contract, which was too small to attract any bids except from universities. Glades won, because it offered not only to develop the program but also to take it directly to growers—which no other bidder offered. Glades desired the contract because it would strengthen its ties with growers with whom it already worked and give it a foot in the door with others. It could also become a profitable sideline. A food-safety program is an ongoing process, so Glades would have ample access to growers. Furthermore, growers would have to undergo food-safety audits, another service Glades provides. So Glades's food-safety activities enhance its consulting, and vice versa.

Now it promotes these points as its competitive advantages:

- Our farm knowledge comes from more than 5,000 farm visits each year and more than thirty years of experience.
- We have delivered food-safety programs to more than 75 percent of the growers in this state, and 98 percent have passed the third-person audits on the first try.
- We are the only food-safety consultants in the state specializing in fresh-produce production systems.
- We have the only hygiene-training video specifically developed for workers in fresh-produce packinghouses.

Moral: Being ahead of your customers' needs not only gives you a competitive advantage over the other guy, it can also open up other lines of business—as long as you can recognize and seize the opportunity.

Banyan Air Service is an FBO (fixed-base operator) located at Ft. Lauderdale Executive Airport. It is a twenty-four-hour, full-service, fixed-base operation serving the Bahamas, the Caribbean, South America, and the southeastern United States. Its CEO is Don Campion, an early convert to the concept of competitive advantage. Some FBOs simply offer fuel and a lobby or resting area for the pilots and passengers using the private airport. Banyan goes the whole nine yards, offering a long list of services for pilots, passengers, and aircraft owners. Among its competitive advantages:

- Voted a Top 10 FBO nationwide for the last seven years.
- Home to 450 aircraft based within the Banyan complex.
- Twenty-four-hour, red-carpet service to more turbine aircraft every day than any other FBO in the Southeast.
- Hangar space always available for most types of aircraft.
- Thirty "Safety First" certified line technicians, seven customer-service representatives, and a large fleet of ground equipment to safely serve you.
- Our avionics division is ranked among the Top 10 in the United States and has installed sixty avionics packages in turbine aircraft over the last twelve months.
- Our technicians meet our promised delivery date 99 percent of the time.
- Our service managers meet or beat the repair quotes 97 percent of the time.
- Our service center is the only independent repair sta-

tion with FAA/JAA, Venezuela, Argentina, and Brazil authorizations and approvals.

- Our maintenance service center was voted in the Top 15 best maintenance facilities in the United States.
- Seventy percent of our customers are referred by other customers.

The son of a missionary, CEO Campion (who prefers the title Coach) grew up in Nigeria, spent a lot of time in small aircraft as a boy, and has been a licensed pilot for decades. In his role as Coach, he doesn't allow any grass to grow on his tarmac—by anticipating and meeting the needs of his customers even before they ask, and by using numbers to reinforce his competitive advantages, he stays high above the competition.

I can't stress enough the importance of measurements. Measurements coupled with a culture dedicated to alignment of competitive advantages and accountability will deliver results every time.

MAKING LEMONADE FROM LEMONS

Any meaningful look at your company is bound to reveal your competitive disadvantages. These are aspects of your business that cry to be fixed, for your competitors can use them against you. But sometimes you can turn even a relatively minor disadvantage into a blue-chip advantage. One of my clients in the office-supply business was hearing that his customers found his staff inaccessible at critical times—even though his competitors were even harder to reach. One option was to do a better job of communicating that he wasn't like his competitors—his staff actually was more accessible. But he came up with a stronger idea. Since it was obvious his customers wanted reassurance that they could contact top management in times of crisis, he gave his personal phone number to his customers and told them they could call him anytime if they had a problem that wasn't being addressed. (To date, only one customer has ever called. And that customer admitted he was only testing to see if he could, indeed, get through to the CEO if he ever needed to.)

At the other end of the scale, you could be saddled with a competitive disadvantage that threatens your very survival—a problem that can't be fixed by simply handing out your personal phone number. In such a case, you have to make major operational changes in order to stay competitive. During the 1990s, the Internet posed a mounting threat to all kinds of businesses, none more than booksellers. Amazon.com put all book retailers at a serious disadvantage, almost overnight. Customers could order discounted books anytime from Amazon, selecting from a vast library, and be assured delivery in a few days. Barnes & Noble took the threat seriously and acted quickly. It started its own online buying service, turning a disadvantage into a healthy revenue stream. Sometimes the best way to turn around a disadvantage is simply to copy the competitor and then try to do him one better, or at least protect your flanks.

Of course, there is a big disadvantage to buying books online—you can't browse the way you can in a real store. So Barnes & Noble decided, in addition to starting an online service, to enhance the book-buying experience at its retail outlets. It put cafés in its bookstores, creating an atmosphere you can't get online.

Your biggest competitive disadvantage could be internal. Perhaps your competition doesn't have a real edge but is gaining ground because something isn't working right in your organization. (If your customers don't know yet, you can bet your competitors do and will be sure to spread the word.)

Xerox Corp. was getting clobbered a few years ago on its own turf—office machines. Its market share was shrinking, even though the competition wasn't offering anything Xerox couldn't match. The problem wasn't the product, or the service, or the price. It was the way Xerox trained its sales force. For years, the company faithfully supplied their clients with copiers and other office machines but didn't spend time talking about new Xerox products and systems. Xerox faced a tough task: to retrain the entire sales staff. It took over two years to do, but Xerox erased an internal competitive disadvantage.

In my workshops, I like to ferret out any perceived competitive disadvantages from the staff in attendance. It is always quite an eye-opener for the CEO. I always ask him or her to remain silent during this phase. The goal is to turn lemons into lemonade.

Sometimes the disadvantages are minor and easily

remedied. At one workshop, employees pointed out that "our trucks aren't clean and new." The solution was simple: clean them at least once a week and replace the fleet over the next couple of years. Even if a move like this does not give you an outright competitive advantage, it can help your brand and image. And the employees will speak better about the company—cleaner, newer trucks and a CEO who listens!

On other occasions, the disadvantage is far more serious. One group noted, "Our employee turnover is so great, our clients never know who they will be speaking to." The CEO was listening and took it to heart. His company invested in better benefits, more incentives, and cross-training to give employees more opportunities. It took years, but it worked. The company's employee-retention rate is now higher than any of its competitors'. Customers like continuity and familiarity.

Another company noted "inconsistent customer contact." The concerned CEO jumped right on the problem. The company created a new policy that directed all sales and service representatives to contact customers at least once a month. Sales began increasing almost immediately.

Here are some other suggestions for creating competitive advantages:

Carve out a new paradigm for your industry. Subway was one of the first fast-food chains to climb on the health-food bandwagon, and it indeed changed its appeal. It began offering low-carb sandwiches and salads using wheat bread, turkey, low-fat dressing, and so on. The idea of healthy hero sandwiches—seemingly an oxymoron—clicked. Subway not only created a competitive advantage over other fast-food competitors, it expanded its universe of customers beyond fast-food junkies.

There are lots of health clubs out there, but if you're a busy woman trying to lose weight and stay fit, how do you determine which is best for you? Curves found an answer with its thirty-minute workouts that many women swear by. Curves is now the largest fitness franchise in the world, with more than 9,000 locations worldwide. It also developed a catchy slogan: "Only one place can give you the strength of over 4 million women."

Dell Computer revolutionized the way people all over the world buy computers by building a business around something old, something new, something borrowed, and something blue. Mail order is as old as the post office. Couple that with online product selection and modification—something new. Dell preloads Microsoft software—something borrowed. And its logo is bold and blue. Marry it all together and you've got a company with revenues of over $50 billion and roughly 58,000 employees around the globe.

A dentist found that many of his aging patients needed implants to anchor their lower plates in place. But such implants are very expensive, more than most retirees would consider spending for a dental procedure. Furthermore, insurers won't cover implants, and recovery takes weeks. So the dentist found an inexpensive yet effective way to cut that cost in half, significantly reduce the pain, and dramatically decrease the healing time by using "temporary" implants. He told me he has a 95 percent success rate and his customers are delighted.

Tout your celebrity status. If you have a list of impressive clients, that might be worth crowing about. Would-be customers feel more secure with a supplier chosen by industry leaders, so if the top ten Fortune 500 companies use your product or service, then say so. This can be especially important for small and medium-size companies without brand visibility. You remember our discussion of JTECH, which makes restaurant pagers? It supplied many major food chains and well-known restaurants with its paging systems and let everyone know it with its slogan: *"Of the fifty largest chains who use paging, 100 percent use JTECH."* No competitor, large or small, could make that claim, and it carries a lot of weight with potential customers.

Reminder: Before you make any investment in touting your impressive client list, do your customer research. Your customers might not be impressed with your list at all. On the other hand, you might discover it's very significant—and worth touting even more loudly.

Brag about your employees' training and experience. Arrow Environmental—the pest-control business I wrote about earlier—tells customers, "Our technicians go through an average of 120 hours of training each year to stay current with changing methods." Constant training may be essential in your industry, but that's no reason to ignore it as a competitive advantage. Even if the competition does the same thing, you can claim it first. Tell your customers how much it costs you. If you tell them you invest half a million dollars a year in technical training, they'll get a better sense of what they are paying for.

Create a solution to a problem your customers face. Recall how MCT Dairies launched a newsletter that keeps its customers informed on trends and prices in the dairy industry. Another of my clients, an office-equipment supplier, provided service on weekends to satisfy the needs of special customers (and wound up attracting a lot of new business, too, especially from law firms that run their copying machines all day and night, seven days a week).

Kill them with a thousand small cuts. Ray Fox ran a business that hardly stirs the blood—a home-appliance service company called Amira Services. Think about it. If you were its CEO, how could you differentiate yourself from the competition?

And please, no generalities like "better service" or "top quality." I'm talking real measurable advantages. By developing a slew of them in as pedestrian a business as you could think of, Ray Fox rates the Jaynie L. Smith award for creativity.

Fox's business was simple. It sold service contracts to repair air conditioners, household appliances, and plumbing and electrical fixtures. If your dishwasher were covered by an Amira contract and it broke down, Amira services would come out and fix it. Amira was in the insurance business, but unlike most insurance companies, its own employees made all the repairs.

Most competitors offered a contract as a package based on all the appliances commonly found in the home. The price was based on the age of the house and increased as the home aged and, presumably, appliances began to break down more frequently.

But Fox's company developed proprietary software called "line item pricing," which allowed the customer to pick and choose which appliances to include in the contract. And if appliances had been replaced since the house was built, the customer with newer appliances got a lower rate, based on the actual age of the insured appliance.

Competitors that tried aggressive pricing against Amira ended up with contracts on houses with old appliances because their package price was never as low as Amira's custom pricing for homes with newer appliances. But that was only the beginning.

The same software analyzed air conditioners with the highest breakdown rates, signaling those likely to fail when the summer season arrived. Amira called customers, requesting permission to take the suspect units out of service for preventive maintenance in the winter, when demand was slow and personnel were underutilized. Since air-conditioning was not critical in the winter, customers were not inconvenienced. But when the heat of summer arrived, the units did not fail. This lowered the demand for service in the summer, which allowed Amira to level out its workload and provide speedier service for those customers whose units did need attention.

The system also tracked all the parts a serviceperson replaced during the day. The servicepeople would call in after every fourth service visit and report the parts he or she had used for repairs. Service personnel kept their trucks at home each night, and each evening they would be sent replacement parts directly from the warehouse by courier along with their work schedule for the next day, so they did not have to stop by the warehouse before starting their workday. Servicepeople were also assigned service areas as close to their homes as possible to reduce travel time and increase productivity. If the serviceperson's regular call area included large condominium complexes, his or her truck would be specially stocked with parts for the brands of appliances that were installed in that complex.

Amira found that it paid to have servicepeople spend a few extra minutes with each customer. Customers liked the attention. To encourage the longer visits, Amira deliberately purchased service vans without air-conditioning. Lingering a few minutes with the customers allowed servicepeople to stay cool a little longer.

Amira's office employees were also cross-trained. Anyone who picked up the phone could schedule service calls, sell a new customer a service contract, check on the status of special-order parts, or provide advice on how to shut down appliances before leaving home for extended periods. Call volume reached its peak on Monday mornings, so at those times the phones were manned by all available personnel—including employees who normally processed payments and contract renewals. With 15 percent more bodies at the phones, customers didn't have to wait to get a live person to handle their requests. Almost 95 percent of all calls were handled by the first person to speak to the customer. The goal was never to leave a customer on hold, despite handling more than 3,000 service calls on a busy day.

The company didn't skimp on parts, either. If a repair could be made with a $10 part but a $20 part was available and deemed to be more reliable or have a longer life, it was always used. The philosophy was that customers were yours for life unless the company ruined the relationship. Better parts produced fewer breakdowns, which meant fewer expensive service calls. On average, materials amounted only to 20 percent of the cost of a service call.

On Christmas and Thanksgiving, the two most critical days of the year for ovens, Amira had enough technicians on standby so no customer had to go without turkey. The company never ceased creating competitive advantages, which drove competitors nuts. At its peak, Amira's renewal rate for service contracts was 97 percent. When Fox took the helm at Amira, the company had 90 employees and $6 million in annual revenue. Seven years later, after strong growth and several acquisitions, annual revenues had reached $60 million, and the company had more than 700 employees.

Fox sold the company, which became Service America

and has since been bought and sold by Roto-Rooter. But it no longer enjoys the competitive advantages it did under Fox—proof that competitive advantages are not permanent and every company should always be striving to come up with new ones.

Remember that competitive advantages are nearly always moving targets. You have to review your own, and your competitors', at least quarterly. Even before the competition starts to mimic you, you should be focused on creating new advantages. Business is a chess game. Play it strategically. You need to think two or three moves ahead if you expect to win.

TURN YOUR DISADVANTAGES INTO COMPETITIVE ADVANTAGES

Evaluating competitive disadvantages is a proven way to uncover and create competitive advantage opportunities.

Ask a large cross section of your employees to name your company's top three disadvantages. Then ask them to offer solutions and brainstorm ideas on how to "fix" these issues. Be sure you let the employees know it is safe to tell the truth. They must be candid; you have to be thick-skinned. Don't shoot the messenger.

Appoint teams to solve problems. Publicly support the team and provide reasonable deadlines.

Keep a sharp eye on your competition. Assess what they are doing better than you. How can you do it better than they can? What investment will you have to make? Is it really important to the customer? Remember, even if your competitors do something better than you, that advantage may not be high on your customers' priority lists. Be sure you check it out before making any major investments.

CHAPTER 10

Communicate, Communicate, Communicate

ONCE YOU HAVE COME UP WITH YOUR LIST OF COM-petitive advantages and have vetted them with your customers, it's time to get the word out. You have to communicate them to your sales staff, other employees, and your existing as well as potential customers.

There are three basic ways of attracting and holding customers. First is through brand awareness. The aim is to condition customers to instinctively buy your product or service because they identify your brand with the product or service you provide. The main vehicle for building a brand is, of course, advertising. There is no disputing the value of brand names, from Coca-Cola and Crest to Microsoft and Intel to H & R Block and Fidelity Investments. Large companies spend millions to advertise and promote their brands and keep them on everyone's minds. They know that customers will choose a familiar name over Brand X. Smaller companies cannot afford that kind of advertising. But that doesn't mean Goliath will always beat David. Keep in mind that no matter how entertaining or catchy the ads, they don't win you customers. You might remember last year's clever Super Bowl ads, but can you name the products they were promoting? Buyers can and do change their buying habits when given good reasons for switching to a competitor's products and services.

The second way to win and keep customers is to maintain a crackerjack sales force that can foster strong relationships with important buyers. This is especially true of small, specialized companies with a limited universe of potential customers. One of my clients has a regional plumbing-supply business and spends as much time entertaining, dining, and playing golf with clients as he does on his business. He considers many of his clients friends. But if a competitor comes along and undercuts him on price, or can provide some other valuable add-ons, those friendships can wither. Those friendly clients will have to put their companies' interests, and their own, ahead of friendship.

If you want to build secure relationships with customers, the third and most effective way to do that is to make sure they know *why* they should buy from you. When you ask them, "Why us?" they should respond with specific reasons—your competitive advantages. Forget brand names or gourmet dinners. Customers who can specify the reasons they are buying from you will stick with you. But it is up to you to provide those advantages, make sure your customers know about them, and keep on developing new competitive advantages to stay ahead of the competition.

How do you communicate your competitive advantages? Early and often. And it starts in your own backyard. First of all, indoctrinate your sales force. They are your storm troopers. They must learn to use your competitive advantages in every sales encounter. They should commit your competitive advantages to memory and translate them into measurable savings in time and costs for your customers. One of my clients listed his company's competitive advantages on small, laminated cards that he gave to all of his salespeople, lest they forget. And they carry a supply of these cards to leave behind with customers and prospects.

Let's say that your company's competitive advantage is prompt delivery of your product. Your sales force should be able to quantify that advantage. They should be able to specify exactly how much money customers can save in inventory, paperwork, employee overhead, administration costs, transportation, and warehousing by buying from you (see Chapter 3).

Every employee sells your business every day in some way. So don't just educate the sales force about what your company is up to; let the rest of the troops know, too. Every key employee on your payroll should be familiar with your competitive advantages, not only because such communication could result in new sales, but also because your employees will be able to better focus on company goals. They're the ones who will be responsible for the measurements and results, so the more they understand the advantages you are promising to deliver, the better they will understand the value of their own performance. One of my clients offers a small cash reward to employees who, when randomly questioned, can tick off the company's top three competitive advantages.

To spread the word about the competitive advantages of which you are now so proud, your first inclination might be to call in an advertising agency and get an ad campaign going. If your budget permits, that is a great idea. Just remember that TV, radio, print, and Internet advertising can all be effective, but they are also expensive and fleeting. Medium-size and small companies with limited ad budgets cannot afford to sustain a big media splash. As important as advertising can be, much of it is lost or ignored, and results are often disappointing. As Jay Conrad Levinson writes in *Guerilla Marketing Excellence,* "Because of the enormous clutter in marketing messages, I'm tempted to suggest that you concentrate *solely* upon your competitive advantages and upon nothing else."

There is always a time and place for advertising, but your audience has to be targeted and your message worth remembering. If you have done a good job creating, uncovering, and articulating your competitive advantages, then an advertising campaign has a better chance of providing your company with a good return on investment.

Before you commit to any new advertising, which will perhaps attract new customers, first make sure that all your existing customers know why they are buying from you. It is far less expensive to retain existing customers than to win new ones. So talk to them before you even think about calling an ad agency. Loyal customers can be important allies in growing your business.

Make full use of all the traditional ways to communicate your message. Start with a new sales brochure that spells out all your competitive advantages, and send it to all your current customers as well as new prospects. Don't just dust off the old brochure with some new language. Design the brochure around the competitive advantages you want to tout. Note: List your competitive advantages in bullet form if you can, instead of paragraphs. Edit your competitive advantages to a few key words for each bullet. They're easier to read and remember. And always lead off with the competitive advantage that is most important in the eyes of the customer (a fact you have confirmed in your customer research, right?).

Devise a memorable phrase or slogan that crystallizes your competitive advantages or otherwise differentiates your company or product, and use it extensively. Perhaps one of your advantages is unique and can stand alone. If you offer free delivery, for example, and your competitors do not, "Always free delivery" would work nicely.

Slogan writing is something of an art, but once a catchy slogan gets into your customers' heads, it sticks. Here are a few slogans from the Ad Slogan Hall of Fame (visit adslogan.com for more). I'll bet you can instantly identify the product or company, even though some of these slogans are many decades old:

"Have it your way." (Burger King, 1973). *"The Citi never sleeps."* (Citibank, 1977). *"Does she or doesn't she?"* (Clairol, 1964). *"Look, Ma, no cavities!"* (Crest, 1958). *"A diamond is forever."* (DeBeers Consolidated, 1948). *"Plop plop, fizz fizz, oh what a relief it is."* (Alka-Seltzer, 1976). *"Capitalist tool."* (Forbes, 1970). *"Guinness is good for you."* (Guinness Breweries, 1929). *"Nothing runs like a Deere."* (John Deere, 1972). *"Good to the last drop."* (Maxwell House, 1915). *"All the news that's fit to print."* (*New York Times*, 1896). *"Where's the beef?"* (Wendy's, 1984). *"Let your fingers do the walking."* (Yellow Pages, 1964).

All of these slogans differentiate products or services. Each conveys a message: from Alka-Seltzer's headache relief to Deere's reliability to the Yellow Pages' convenience. You don't have to be an advertising copywriter to come up with a good slogan. You might even stage a contest among employees or customers to come up with the best slogan.

Use your slogan on all your company literature, including letterhead, posters, newsletters, fax cover letters, e-mail signatures, and invoices, and on your delivery trucks. Add it to your "on hold" telephone message. Print it on all your employees' business cards. Anything your customer receives from you or sees and hears when doing business with you presents an opportunity to get your message across. Don't let these opportunities go to waste. They are there for the taking. Some companies even imprint their messages on napkins. Every cocktail napkin on Continental Airlines, for example, delivers this line: "More flights to more destinations."

Wherever you have a captive audience, you have a chance for your message to get special attention, especially if there is nothing else around for folks to read. When you board a Continental flight, you see the following message printed on the airplane fuselage, at the eye level of boarding passengers: "SixSuccess: Fortune Best Place to Work Six Years in a Row." Best place to work means happy employees, and happy employees mean a better customer experience.

If clients visit your company, make good use of your waiting area. You don't have to hang a garish banner across your building lobby (as the ill-fated Enron once did with "The World's Leading Company"), but tasteful use of a slogan beneath your logo at the receptionist's desk can be memorable.

Some chain restaurants use place mats to tell the stories of their companies. And they often sell extra ad space on the place mats to other businesses, for cash or barter. It can be an effective and inexpensive ad buy for you. Note: Don't overlook your own packaging as a medium for your message. We all know how kids (and grown-ups, too) become absorbed in whatever is printed on cereal boxes.

If your customers spend any time at all looking at the

packaging of your product—and they often do—you have an excellent opportunity to deliver your message. Here's what Cape Cod Potato Chip Co. prints on the bags of its reduced-fat chips:

> In early 1995 we set out to create a reduced fat chip that would maintain the integrity of our classic chip. The chips inside this bag are not fabricated potato crisps made from dehydrated potato flakes nor do they contain any bizarre fat substitutes. These chips contain only select potatoes from regional potato farms, vegetable oil and salt.

Note how the message rips the competition and distances itself from "fabricated potato crisps made from dehydrated potato flakes." I'll bet most potato-chip fanciers don't have a clue as to how their favorite chips are made, but Cape Cod tells you. The company even invites you on a free tour of its chipping plant in Hyannis, Massachusetts. You'll get a free bag of chips for your trouble, and learn all kinds of neat things about the company and how it makes its potato chips. (It takes four pounds of potatoes to make a pound of chips, for example.) Factory tours can be excellent showcases for your company and your products.

Make sure the promotional gifts and novelties that you give away contain your slogan or chief competitive advantage. I still have a ski hat from a resort in Alta, Utah, that is noted for its deep powder and relatively low prices. The line on the hat, "Still deeper, still cheaper," stays with me—I still go back to Alta. Companies that give away promotional pens, calculators, golf balls, and so on, that carry only the company logo are missing a great opportunity.

THE INTERNET CONNECTION

One of the greatest tools for reaching and impressing your customers, new and old, is your strategically designed Web site. But it seems the word has been slow to get around. I'm convinced that one day several years ago, all the CEOs of all the companies in the world simultaneously announced to their subordinates: "Damn it! This is the electronic age! Let's get us a Web site! Now!"

How else could you account for the fact that so many Web sites are so boringly similar? Before every presentation I make, I check out the Web sites of the companies whose executives will be in attendance. First, I look for examples of what a good one should include. I seldom find any. Too many Web sites look as if they were cobbled together in a day or so and resemble tired sales handouts. When I single out one of those Web sites to illustrate what *not* to do, I often am greeted with a sea of red faces. Executives of the cited company are embarrassed, and so are most of the others. They know their Web sites are no better and fear they will be singled out next.

Too often, Web sites are slapped together by committee—or, worse yet, by an information technology executive who has never taken a marketing course. If you run your company, make it your business to have an outstanding site. Appoint one of your sharper lieutenants to handle it. Your Web site is your showcase to the world. Even if you don't sell directly over the Internet, your Web site could be the cheapest, most effective way of communicating and marketing. It's your pipeline to old and new customers, as well as anyone else interested in your company—from stockholders and analysts to prospective employees. And creating a powerful Web site won't cost you any more than throwing together a weak, boring one.

If you own a small business and you don't yet have a full-blown Web site, make it a priority. There is no excuse today for a simple billboard site containing the excuse "Our new Web site is currently under construction." You could be losing customers every day it's under construction. And bear this in mind: Content is king, not design. It is up to you to decide what information you want on your site, and you should give it a lot of thought. Don't simply ape your competitors (although there is nothing wrong with modeling your site after highly successful sites). If you cannot afford to hire a Web site designer, enlist some online help from sites like register.com. or homestead.com. They provide one-stop shopping—from registering your domain name to designing your site to hosting it and handling your e-mail traffic—all for a reasonable fee. And you never have to leave your office.

The most important part of the Web site, however, is still up to you—the content. Web sites that try to do too much are confusing. And a confusing site looks like a confused company. As always, put yourself in the shoes of your customers. What do they care about? Garry McGovern and Rob Norton have written a highly praised guide for managers and Web writers who have to decide what content to put on Web sites. The authors maintain that readers (they refuse to call them "users") want seven things when they visit your Web site:

- Readers want to be able to find things.
- Readers want your advice.
- Readers want up-to-date, quality content.
- Readers want relevant and straightforward content.
- Readers want to do things.
- Readers want to interact.
- Readers want privacy.

Their book, *Content Critical: Gaining Competitive Advantage Through High-Quality Web Content* (Financial Times Prentice Hall, 2001), will help you decide what information you should have on your site and what you shouldn't.

Take a look at your existing Web site. Chances are it includes an "About Us" section. It seems that almost every company site on the Internet has one. It often pictures a few balding men, perhaps a woman or two, and some history of the company and the folks who run it. Do your readers care? Stash that information somewhere else on the site, or scrap it completely. Your "About Us" section should give readers a capsule description of the company's business, not its history or the pedigrees of the principals. It should list your competitive advantages. Here's an example of what an "About Us" section *should* say. It's from theperfumeshop.com., and it answers the question "Why us?"

Impartial Advice—Great Prices— 117 Stores + Online

The Perfume Shop is the UK's largest specialist fragrance retailer—with 117 stores nationwide.

We only sell perfume and related products—with over 1000 products to choose from. So we offer impartial advice, great prices and the most comprehensive collection.

Some leading brands don't yet allow official sales on the net (we are working on them!) so on-line we always suggest alternative brands.

Click here to find your nearest store.

There you have a clear, simple statement of why customers should buy at The Perfume Shop—in less than 100 words. Bravo! I advise clients to completely scrap their "About Us" sections and rename them "Why Us?" sections. It is the perfect venue for you to articulate your competitive advantages (though they should be spread liberally throughout your entire Web site). Make the "Why Us?" page the first click on your Web site with a bullet-point list of your competitive advantages.

If you can't bring yourself to abandon the pictures of

the company picnic, the lists of alma maters, and the little vignette about starting the company in an abandoned warehouse, a dead-end street, or a rotting pier, at least have your "Why Us?" page pop up first.

Your Web site should also have a number of links to other businesses, which in turn should link back to you. A building-supply company, for example, should include links to the manufacturers of tools and building equipment. They, in turn, should list the building company among those featuring their products. Remember, the more hits you get on your site, the higher it will rank on Google's and other search engines' lists.

Some Web sites make it easy for readers to send e-mail messages directly to company executives by name. But this tactic can backfire; you could wind up fielding a slew of complaints and kook-mail. Direct customers to send comments and inquiries to appropriate departments, not individual people. But make sure your best customers have your e-mail address.

Give some thought to advertising on Google and other search engines. It will give your company more visibility.

CREATING BUZZ ON A BUDGET

Once your Web site is in place, with your competitive advantages prominently displayed, you want to generate as much traffic as you can to that site, as well as to your offices and showrooms. How can you create some buzz about your company without spending a fortune on advertising? The short answer is: Any way you can (as long as it's legal and helps business).

A few months ago, I ran across an article in *Business-Week* that described the steps taken by a new publication called *The Week* to attract attention and generate sales. Not all of the tricks that the publisher employed will work in every business, but the example should suggest some good ideas. Most of them are not new, but all are brilliantly executed.

Like a businessman's *Reader's Digest, The Week* enjoys a distinctive competitive advantage of rival publications: brevity. *The Week* has no reporters and no writers, because all of its content comes from other publications. Articles are taken and chopped from numerous sources by a small team of sharp editors. The digest, launched in 2001, is aimed at top executives and other U.S. leaders who are hard-pressed for time to read all the publications that they need to. *The Week* does the culling for them, and delivers the key articles in bite-size portions, for $75 a year.

The problem: How do you reach the target market? How can you get the word out to folks who are already too busy to read what they need to read? The traditional route for launching new publications is through advertising and direct mail, very expensive and risky options, especially when targeting affluent readers.

The management at *The Week* decided to let the publication speak for itself, by sending free subscriptions to well-known people in business, the arts, and politics. But with a catch. In return for the freebie subscription, readers were asked to write a few kind words about the publication. Each week, some of the testimonials are then printed on the cover of the magazine. Among the blurb writers: Yahoo! CEO Terry Semel, UBS chairman Don Marron, Barry Goldwater, Jr., and Mario Cuomo. Woody Allen wrote that the magazine "was for movers and shakers, and I can't stop shaking."

The Week began to catch on as word of mouth spread, fueled by its celebrity subscribers. In 2004, circulation approached 300,000 copies, and advertising revenue grew by 66 percent over the previous year. *The Week* bucked the trend of the falling ad revenues that plagued the established newsweeklies—the same periodicals from which it swipes some of its copy. Most publications don't mind the lifts, as long as they are attributed. In fact, some publications deliberately try to get *The Week* to publish excerpts.

In keeping with its elitist image, *The Week* also bucked another trend by reducing, not expanding, its advertising hole—space devoted to ad pages. Ads occupy only 30 percent of its pages, while most publications average close to 50 percent ads. With fewer ad pages, *The Week* can charge more dollars per page, and advertisers are willing to pay for a less cluttered magazine that has a better chance of grabbing the attention of its upscale readership.

The Week didn't stop there. It hooked up with some highly respected organizations to sponsor forums and meetings, including the Conference Board and the Aspen Institute. It hosts CEO breakfast forums and holds an annual opinion forum to honor columnists and writers. More buzz. Give a writer a prize and he'll never stop bragging about it.

The brilliance of *The Week*'s strategy lay in letting its high-profile customers do the talking. Readers supply the testimonials; they tote the magazine around; they quote from it; they attend its breakfasts and seminars. And most are happy to pay the full $75 a year for it when their free subscriptions run out.

Gift subscriptions are common in magazine publishing. Ad agencies never pay for magazines, for example. But by soliciting its elite readers' opinions—and plastering the best of them on its cover—*The Week* got an extraordinary amount of mileage out of its gift subscriptions.

Can you turn your best customers into salesmen for your company? Absolutely. Even if their names aren't Woody Allen or Mario Cuomo, and you're not offering them free cover space.

PUTTING YOUR CUSTOMERS TO WORK

Have you ever been so delighted—or annoyed—with something you've bought that you want to sit down and write a letter to the president of the company? I once bought a barbecue grill on mail order. Though it was advertised as "easily assembled," I had to hire my handyman to put it together. It took him about two hours. In other words, not so easily assembled. As he sweated through the grill's assembly, I composed a letter in my head to the CEO that went something like this:

> Dear CEO:
> Have you ever put together one of your damned grills? Have you ever actually read the assembly instructions? Do you like to pull the wings off flies?
> Sincerely,
> Jaynie Smith

I never wrote or sent the letter, of course, but I have been bad-mouthing that grill for years. I would never buy another or recommend it to anyone.

On the other hand, when I changed doctors a while back for one in the MDVIP program (see Chapter 6), I was so pleased that I thought of dropping a note to its CEO singing its praises. I didn't, but I do recommend MDVIP to friends and colleagues every chance I get.

I am sure that I am not alone. Most folks just don't volunteer their dissatisfaction to CEOs unless they are really bent out of shape. And they don't write fan letters, either, unless they have some sort of epiphany. Yet happy customers can generate word of mouth and send it zipping through the marketplace like a chain letter. In their very useful book *Creating Customer Evangelists: How Loyal Customers Become a Volunteer Sales Force* (Dearborn Trade, 2002), authors Ben McConnell, Jackie Huba, and Guy Kawasaki describe how companies like Krispy Kreme and Southwest Airlines and IBM create and coddle fan clubs, give them discounts or freebies, throw parties for them, and urge them to spread the gospel far and wide.

That's fine for big companies with very large customer bases and hefty marketing budgets. But what about small or medium businesses, or those whose products or services are not used by millions? They are only looking for a few important customers to start and sustain buzz. How do you turn them into evangelists?

Enter the customer advisory board. That is, a group of important customers who tell the company what they think is good and bad about it. They can supply important customer feedback to the decision makers at an organization.

But in recent years, some companies, large and small, have created customer advisory boards for a different reason: to turn important customers into unpaid consultants and salespeople. The authors of *Creating Customer Evangelists* cite several companies that have been particularly successful with consumer boards. Paetec Corp., for example, is a Northeast telecommunications company that provides integrated communications, including local and long-distance voice services, data and Internet services, software applications, and so on.

Paetec wanted to make sure that what it was developing and selling was what the market wanted. Normal customer research just didn't yield enough information, so Paetec turned to a consultant, PeerHQ in Rochester, New York, to help set up consumer advisory boards and arrange meetings. In November 2003, the company tested three boards in three cities, and the results were so positive it created ten boards and has nine more in development, with more than 100 board members signed up so far.

Board members receive no financial compensation, but they do get the chance to network with other board members. They get to pick one another's brains. At meetings, half of the time is reserved for board members to share ideas and discuss their own business problems. That kind of compensation is worth a lot more to the members than a small paycheck. "There's an equal-person feeling to all the meetings, because we all share the same issues," said one board member. They are helping their own companies, and helping themselves, by helping Paetec.

The company listens to what they say. Board members convinced Paetec to delay the rollout of a new marketing program until it could be redesigned to accommodate members' comments and suggestions. They have also assisted in the design and testing of new products. And they are all strong ambassadors of Paetec. Communications sometimes turns into marketing, which is not a bad thing.

A DEPARTING NOTE

One more thought before I leave you to get back to business. I'm convinced, because I have seen it happen so often, that the competitive advantage strategy I've outlined here really works. It will work for you as long as you make a strong commitment to see it through and do frequent follow-ups. As with any business, success simply doesn't happen by accident; you have to make it happen. As Jim Collins put it in *Good to Great* (Collins, 2001):

> The good to great companies were not, by and large, in great industries and some were in terrible industries. In no case do we have a company that just happened to be sitting on the nose cone of a rocket when it took off. Greatness is not a function of circumstance. Greatness, it turns out, is largely a matter of conscious choice.

GET THE WORD OUT

Make a list of all of your company's communication vehicles: advertising, brochures, business cards, signage, videos, trucks, and so on. Be sure to highlight your competitive advantages everywhere you possibly can.

Review your Web site. Make sure your first hit is a "Why Us?" page. You may have only one chance to get your prospects' attention. Slam-dunk them with this "Why Us?" page.

Make sure your company establishes a competitive advantage review so that your "greatness can be a conscious choice." I recommend monthly review meetings where you go over many of the questions posed in the exercise sections of this book.

Designate a Chief Competitive Advantage Officer who holds everyone accountable for the monthly review, establishes competitive advantage metrics, gathers competitive intelligence on the competition, commissions market research, and promotes customer advisory boards.

Who in your company works closely with marketing and sales to ensure that the company's competitive advantages are stated in its communications? Do you have any way to ensure the proper use of competitive advantage statements while on sales calls? Who is in charge of looking for new competitive advantages in your company? Are you including competitive advantage review in your strategic planning exercises?

Note: Sometimes a savvy, objective outsider can help you ferret out your competitive advantages. You need fresh eyes asking the right questions. Consider hiring a seasoned consultant who is not terribly familiar with your organization—but who does understand strategic planning, operational decision-making, and their impact on marketing and sales.

It takes time and effort to get everyone in your company on the bandwagon, but it pays off. I hope this book will inspire you to make that effort, and that it can serve as a guide to making the most of your competitive advantages. Good luck and great prosperity to readers one and all.

Note to readers: I would very much like to hear your competitive advantage success stories. Please share your story with me so I can include your company in my next book. You can contact me at my Web site, www.smartadvantage. com.

Index